T0193459

ENUANI

*Tales, Traits, and Proverbs of a Traditional
African Culture in Transition*

by

INNO CHUKUMA ONWUEME,
MALIJE ONWUEME

authorHOUSE®

AuthorHouse™
1663 Liberty Drive
Bloomington, IN 47403
www.authorhouse.com
Phone: 1 (800) 839-8640

This is a work of fiction. Names, characters, places and incidents either are the product of the author's imagination or are used fictitiously, and any resemblance to any actual persons, living or dead, events, or locales is entirely coincidental.

Published by AuthorHouse 02/28/2019

ISBN: 978-1-7283-0026-9 (sc)
ISBN: 978-1-7283-0025-2 (hc)
ISBN: 978-1-7283-0024-5 (e)

Library of Congress Control Number: 2019901701

Print information available on the last page.

This book is printed on acid-free paper.

Dedication

Dedicated to Peace and Prosperity of

ENUANI

**And its People,
Plus their Well-wishers
Throughout the World.**

✿ **Ma onye alachana mgbemgbe ọnụ a, ụgwụlụ analị a ya**
[Enuani proverb: If you abandon your own lips
by not licking them, the dry Harmattan wind
will take over and snatch them from you]

Contents

☼ Chapter 1

Introduction [Nnụa]

Who are the Enuani People?

Enuani people are the indigenous inhabitants of the following local government areas in Delta State, Nigeria: Aniocha North, Aniocha South, Oshimili North and Oshimili South (see map in Appendix). The people are sometimes referred to as Aniocha/Oshimili, but these terms are of more recent origin, and are more political than the historical traditional name, Enuani. Enuani people speak Igbo-related dialects, intelligible to the broader Igbo linguistic groups east of the Niger River. Enuani forms a sub-set of Anioma (previously called Western Ibo, Bendel

Ibo, or Delta Ibo), the collective term that also includes the Ika and Ndokwa people.

Even though a few riverine towns in Aniocha/Oshimili have historically not identified themselves as Enuani, the term has evolved, for lack of a better comprehensive name, as a term to cover all of Aniocha/Oshimili. Admittedly, other definitions and understandings of Enuani certainly exist. But as a working definition, Enuani in this book refers to all the people of Aniocha/ Oshimili, their territory, their language, and their culture. For simplicity, we have used the word **Enuani** throughout this book, even though the accurate pronunciation is **Enuànį**.

Rationale for this work: Intended Goals and Beneficiaries

The number of Enuani people living outside the Enuani geographical area keeps increasing from generation to generation. These are people with Enuani parental heritage who find themselves living elsewhere within Nigeria, or in various parts of the world. Some of them are raising children who are at risk of losing all meaningful contact with Enuani culture and language. How can such diaspora Enuani people keep in touch with their language and culture?

Even within the Enuani area, there are Enuani youth who have some contact with Enuani proverbs and tales, but do not fully understand what they mean or how to use them. How can we help such curious young people towards a deeper understanding of their language and culture?

With the increasing encroachment of modernity, how can we preserve and archive the traditional proverbs and story-telling that have historically been the backbone of Enuani diction?

Enuani was historically not a written language. Linguistic studies of it are very scarce. With this scarcity, how can we provide additional material for linguists who wish to study Enuani language?

Given the above questions, the goals of this work are to:

1.   Provide diaspora Enuani people and home-based youth with a tool for improving their knowledge of Enuani language and culture;

2.   Assist budding Enuani speakers to enrich their diction with Enuani proverbs and tales;

3.   Document, explore, explain and archive Enuani proverbs and tales in the face of the fact that many of them are dying out;

4.   Demonstrate how Enuani proverbs are used, through examples and explanations;

5.   Peer into the character traits of Enuani people, and examine daily lives in traditional Enuani society;

6.   Show how proverbs, aphorisms, and tales serve as a window on the culture, posture, nature, and future of Enuani, while reflecting how the proverbs are related to traditional Enuani society;

7.   Provide valuable material for linguists, anthropologists, ethnographers, and other academics pursuing studies of Enuani people, language and culture;

8.   Promote interest and competency in Enuani matters among Enuani people and the general population;

9.   Examine the impact of modernity on various aspects of Enuani culture;

10. Stimulate persons of other ethnicities to undertake similar deep explorations into their own proverbs, tales, and culture.

If you are not from Enuani, what is the value of this book to you? What is in it for you? Surely, you identify with one of the thousands of ethnic groups around the world. Our fervent hope is that what we are doing with Enuani will inspire you to do something similar to promote and preserve the culture with which you identify. As a bonus, you get an insight into the nature and culture of Enuani people.

Perspective and Scope

While working towards the goals stated above, this book is targeted at a global audience, including many who are not Enuani indigenes, or who have very little knowledge of the language. It should also provide useful material for academic research into all aspects of Enuani life.

Given that both authors are professionals in the sciences, we lay no claim to expertise in linguistics, anthropology, or related fields. We approach this work essentially as highly motivated amateurs. But as true indigenes of Enuani, we assert our birthright to Enuani culture and proverbs. We will do what we can to deepen understanding of the culture, and promote the use of these proverbs.

The culture of Enuani people is not static. It does not stand still. Instead, it is dynamic, evolving with the social and political winds that batter the Enuani people. As such, any discussion of the language and culture is circumscribed by a time frame. In the case of this book, the perspective is from the first two decades of the 21st century, looking back and looking forward. It is a time when Enuani seems disproportionately occupied with the past which cannot be changed, while ignoring opportunities to formulate strategic options for a brighter future.

This book has employed several methods to delve into the Enuani culture and condition. The first method (Section I, Tales) follows the age-old Enuani tradition of using tales and their morals to make a point. We have included three such tales for their insightful description of Enuani culture and situation. Each tale explores the interesting interplay between the age-old traditional culture in Enuani and the more modern Western culture that has been quietly encroaching since the colonial era. As the tales clearly show, the two cultures are engaged in a clasping dance with each other, a dance sometimes resembling the aggressive grappling of a wrestling match. While the setting of each tale is within Enuani, each of the tales is original in the sense that it was developed and told for the first time by us, the authors of this book. They are therefore not folk tales in the usual sense of tales handed down through generations. Each tale is an independent, self-contained short story.

The second method (Section II, Traits) is a direct essay exposé style which presents arguments and points in a straightforward manner. The subject matters chosen are Enuani language, ethos, and food systems.

The third method that this book uses to examine Enuani culture is through proverbs and aphorisms (Section III). The Section opens with information on how Enuani dialect is spoken and written. Then, over ten dozen Enuani proverbs are subjected to detailed analysis, with literal translations, figurative translations, explanations, examples, and commentary for each one.

Hopefully, this mixture of presentation methods will enrich your reading experience, while challenging you to deeper thought.

Here's a note about the English used in this book, especially in the dialogues. Given their background, the characters presented in the tales would not be conversing in English at all, not even in Pidgin English. They would be talking in the Enuani dialect. As such, the conversations presented are indeed translations into English, with an emphasis on conveying the correct meaning. Much of it is rendered in simple English, but in some cases, the full flavor of meaning demands more complex phraseology. In contrast to the essay chapters on Enuani Traits (Section II), a deliberate effort has been made to simplify the English in the Tales (Section I).

Some portions of this book have been adapted from previous publications by the same authors. Such segments have been embellished and significantly improved, while their appearance in this book makes for greater accessibility.

Where generic gender references such as "him/her" occur in this work, we have mostly opted to use either "him" or "her", on the understanding that any other gender is equally represented. Hopefully, this makes for smoother reading than constantly repeating "him/her" or "he/she".

Acknowledgments

While many of the images used in this book are our own original photographs, some are from the pexels.com website. Pexels is an open source which explicitly states that their pictures require no attribution/royalties/permission, and can be used for commercial and non-commercial purposes. All the same, we wish to acknowledge them for providing this service.

Various relatives and friends have offered immense support in the process of this work. We specifically thank Olabisi Falana, Bundo Onwueme, Onyeka Obodoako, and Ebele Onwueme, for their valuable support and contributions. We are grateful to Dr. Matt Mogekwu for his interest and useful discussions regarding Enuani proverbs. Similarly, we are indebted to our forefathers and foremothers for upholding Enuani proverbs and story-telling through a vibrant oral tradition that has endured for ages.

☼ **SECTION I** ☼

Enuani Tales [Sị M Ịtà]

☼ Chapter 2

Weekend Worries Waylay Keli

With all the world's problems piled up on his shoulders, Keli's middle name might as well be Atlas. Nobody called him that. Nobody dared to. But they wouldn't be wrong if they did. As deputy director at the foreign ministry, how much more of the country's load could Keli carry? Then add to that, his position as the eldest son, and only college graduate, of his kindred back in Alaku, his home village. Whether in the office or in the village, everybody looked up to him for guidance or advice or support. That's Mr. Atlas, if ever there was one.

And talking about names, what sort of name was *Keli* anyway? It certainly was not a name commonly found among his Enuani people. When he was born, his parents named him Okolie. This was a common Enuani name for male children born on *Olie* day (which along with *Afo, Nkwo,* and *Eke* constituted the Enuani traditional four-day "week" cycle). Theoretically, a quarter of male Enuani children could be named Okolie. It was not surprising, therefore, that Keli had several cousins named Okolie, not to mention numerous other persons around Alaku. He was content with the name in early childhood. But the contentment didn't last, as he progressively realized that many people shared the name with him. One of those who shared the name was the catechist at the local Catholic church. Everybody in the village knew the catechist by the name Okolie. But the missionary Irish parish priest struggled with the name, and simply called his catechist Keli. Our child Okolie heard the modified name and liked it. By the age of five, he was already encouraging his relatives to call him Keli.

At the mature age of seven, Keli's mother took him to be enrolled in the village primary school. His mother told them that his name was Okolie. But Keli insisted otherwise. He told the teacher point blank that his name was Keli. His illiterate mother, totally alien in the school environment, had no appreciation of the implications of the written name. So, she gave in to Keli's wish without a fight.

The inscription of Keli's new name in the school register marked his first tentative step in his journey into the new Western culture that represented modernity. The name Keli stuck, and followed him through thousands of similar steps of cultural transformation into the new culture. For a lifetime, his persona alternated between Okolie and Keli. Between the dutifully docile son of the traditional village, and the wizened wizard of the modern world in the city.

Keli's embrace of modernity did not stop with his first name. Somewhere down the road, he decided that his family name, Alilio, was too staid. Never mind that in Enuani dialect, Alilio meant Prayer, a good thing. Keli was looking for something more jazzy and more modern. If the first name and the surname could rhyme, that would be a bonus. So, the last letter in his surname was allowed to fade away, to make room for the emergence of Keli Alili. The new name combination certainly had a nice ring of both modernity and symmetry. And rhyme. Certainly more hip than Okolie Alilio. It's true that the new surname had the unflattering meaning of Remorse in Enuani dialect. But Keli didn't care. He'd found a name he liked, and that was it.

So it was that only a few villagers back home knew Keli's original names. To everyone else, to the wider world, and in all his official documents, he was simply Keli Alili.

Atlas or not, Keli, too, needed guidance and advice. Of late, numerous personal problems were making his life a nightmare. For guidance and emotional recharge, he decided to travel to Alaku from his city abode in Magotown. By spending the weekend in Alaku, he hoped to find the bucolic peace necessary to think clearly and reset his bearings. Advice and emotional support from his father would be an added bonus. His six-year old son, Bedemu, accompanied him on the trip.

Keli and Bedemu arrived in Alaku on Friday evening. The relatives welcomed them in a flurry of excitement, with many remarking how much Bedemu had grown since their last visit home. Having no house of his own in the village, Keli was obliged to lodge in his cousin's half-finished bungalow, a short distance from his father's old family home. Keli retired early for the night, but not before arranging to meet with his father just before dawn. Bedemu stayed back at the family home, to spend the night with his grandfather.

Keli slept soundly for the first part of the night. But, as night dragged on towards dawn, his sleep became progressively less peaceful. All kinds of thoughts wrestled with sleep and fought it to a standstill. Profound thoughts, profane thoughts, peaceful thoughts, petrifying thoughts; all kept him awake as they battled for turf in his disturbed mind. He woke up several times to check his watch to make sure he was punctual for his appointment with his father. For him, this appointment was the most important item on his agenda for this weekend visit to Alaku. Life in Magotown, where he lived and worked, was exciting enough, and the weekends were even more so. But a weekend back home to confer with his father was all he needed. A priceless recharging of his spiritual batteries.

By 5 a.m., Keli could already hear his father's stirrings in the old family house. He got up, scooped some water from the drinking pot, and washed his face vigorously. That water did the hygienic cleaning, but it also washed away any lingering remnants of sleep. He used the last of the water to rinse his mouth. He figured he was now as presentable as he needed to be for this time of day. Feeling clean and fully awake, he headed for the main house. As he passed through the veranda in the main house, he evoked an uproarious crackling cackle from the chicken that were sleeping there. They were not done sleeping, and apparently did not welcome Keli's rude intrusion.

Keli entered the family house through the unlocked back door. Though he opened it gingerly, the old door still protested with a creaky squeak as Keli opened and closed it. The quietness of the household and the stillness of the morning combined to magnify the rude utterances of the noisy door.

Keli tiptoed towards the living room. To his surprise, Ojiso, his father, was already seated there, partially pensive and partially trying to shake off the lingering remnants of the night's sleep. The air hung thick with the smell of burning kerosene, emanating from the hurricane lantern that stood on the corner table. As was usual, the lantern had burned on a low setting all night. Ojiso did not bother to turn up the lantern, as he waited for Keli. So, Keli walked into a living room that was bathed in the eerie glow of semi-darkness. All was silent, except for the rhythmic snoring from an adjoining room.

Keli walked in and greeted his father in the formal, traditional way.

"Okpa, Baa," he greeted, standing squarely in front of his father and pounding his clenched right fist into his open left palm.

"*Daalu*. Thank you, my child," Ojiso responded, nodding his head in approval. "Did you sleep well?"

Keli repeated the greeting two more times, with a similar response from his father. Once the greetings were over, Keli took a seat close to Ojiso. Most of the household was still asleep, so the two needed to sit close to each other to enable them to converse in hushed tones.

Save us from our in-law's claws

As Keli settled down to confer with his father, he fully expected to hear something about the need for him to erect a house in the village, a way of declaring his manhood to Alaku. Building such a house was a recurrent refrain in his discussions with his father in recent years. This topic always irritated Keli, and his father knew it. But Ojiso also knew that the only way to get action on this matter was to keep pounding it into Keli's head.

Ojiso did not disappoint. Keli's lack of effort to build a village house was definitely on the agenda. But first, there were a few more pressing family matters to dispose of. The most pressing one had to do with Uju, Keli's younger sister. Uju had only been married a few years, but she was having serious marital problems. Basically, her husband turned out to be a spouse abuser, subjecting Uju to physical torment at the slightest provocation. Uju tolerated the situation to the limits of her endurance.

"Uju seems to be having such a rough time in this her marriage," Ojiso said.

"So it seems."

"It was only seven weeks ago that they had a major crisis, before this one."

"I wasn't aware of that crisis," replied Keli.

"Oh, yes. I didn't want to disturb you by contacting you in Magotown. Moreover, I think you were on an overseas trip then with the minister."

"Yes. The minister's always dragging me everywhere he goes. He thinks he needs the deputy director for everything."

"Anyway, about seven weeks ago, I was just sitting here one Sunday afternoon. Then a message arrived that Uju had run away, after fighting with her husband overnight."

"She didn't run to you here at home?" Keli asked.

"No. She went to the home of her husband's uncle. As you know, running to her husband's relatives is a sign of respect for them, and gives them a chance to try to sort things out."

"Good."

"It's as if she's lodging a complaint to her husband's relatives about her husband's misdeeds. Handling the matter within the husband's family protects the husband's honor in the eyes of outsiders. It shows that she's not seeking to abandon the marriage."

"So, what did the husband's uncle do?" asked Keli.

"Well, he and a couple of other elders waded into the matter. They scolded Uju's husband for his bad temper. They made him promise never to physically threaten Uju again. So, after about three days, Uju returned to her husband."

"It now seems that the settlement didn't work," suggested Keli.

"Not from the look of things. Indeed, things look much worse now."

"How?"

"When she fled last week, Uju didn't run to her husband's relatives. She ran back to our home here; her paternal home. According to our tradition, this means that the situation is grave. Very grave. She seems to have given up on the husband's relatives."

"And possibly on the husband as well," said Keli.

"Possibly. But that would be a great pity. All other aspects of the marriage seemed to be going well. If only this curse of spousal abuse could be eliminated from it, things could be quite rosy. They've been blessed in many ways. Look at their three beautiful children."

"Yes. I really feel for those children. As our people say, *Nwa bụ isi*; the welfare of the children is paramount in the family. I'm sure all this discord must be affecting Uju's children. Did she bring them when she ran here last week?"

"No. She only brought the youngest one who is not yet weaned," Ojiso said.

"Those children are all suffering. But it would be even worse for them if Uju left the husband completely... So, where is Uju now?"

"As expected, her fleeing was secret but sudden. She left all her belongings behind. Anyway, she spent only one night here. She went on to stay with your mother's relatives in the next town. She said she wanted to escape the attention of prying Alaku villagers, especially her husband's relatives."

"Do you know where she is, in case we want to get in touch?" asked Keli.

"I know precisely where she is. And right now, I suspect she's on the lookout for any message from us. Especially messages regarding any moves by her husband's relatives."

"Yes. I was going to ask you. Have they made any moves?"

"Nothing significant. The day after Uju fled, they sent a delegation here to ask after her. But emotions were still running too high for any meaningful discussions to take place."

"So, what do you think?" Keli asked.

"Well, it's very fortunate that you're here this weekend. You can help me and Uju to formulate a response to our in-laws. What's your own thinking?"

"I think that we must continue to search for reconciliation, if only for the sake of the children. We must find a solution that permits Uju to go back with good assurances of safety, respect, and happiness."

There was silence for about a minute, while each person presumably searched for ideas on how to handle Uju's marital problem.

"You know that in my job as deputy director, I often go round giving lectures," Keli said, breaking the long silence, and seeming to change the topic.

"I know. You government people are full of talk-talk," replied Ojiso, unsure what connection this had with Uju's situation.

"Yes. But we talk sense most of the time."

"That's what you think, but I'm not sure everybody agrees."

"Anyway, just two months ago, I was invited to give a talk at the college that my wife Dada attended."

"The Teachers' College in Magotown?"

"Yes. And do you know what they asked me to speak about?"

"Tell me," inquired Ojiso.

"Spousal abuse. That was the topic they gave me. Spousal abuse. I spoke to them at length about its evils, how it shows a lack of respect for the abused spouse, and how it is the number one cause of marriage breakdown in our society."

"Yes, it's such a common thing these days," Ojiso stated. "In my time, we used to respect our women a lot. I've had major disagreements with your mother, but I've never punched her. These days, you young men are so tense all the time. You work out your frustrations on your wives and use them as punching bags."

"Not all of us."

"Not all, but many. Too many. I don't know why your generation is so inclined to violence against your spouses. Of course, in earlier times, our society practiced polygamy. We could always marry another wife if the first one proved incompatible. Maybe that allowed us to be a bit more tolerant. We did not feel trapped with one person."

"You think people beat their wives because they feel trapped?" asked Keli.

"Not really; but who knows? That may be part of it. Since marrying another wife is out of the question for young people today, they feel trapped and frustrated. They become violent. The only alternative that they see is divorce. And that's a terrible alternative, because of what it does to the children. It tears them apart emotionally, socially, psychologically. It tears them apart in all ways."

"You're right, Baa," Keli agreed. "That's the way I see Uju's case too. If not for the hardship it would inflict on the three children, I would have long ago asked Uju to leave her marriage; to divorce that brute she has as a husband. But can you imagine those three children growing up without their father or without their mother?"

"That's why some people say that divorce is an answer that generates questions. It's a solution that creates problems. It provides an easy solution for the spouses, but generates problems for the children."

"It's like passing on the burden from the adults to the children," added Keli. "That's why I think that divorce should only be used as a last resort."

"But," asked Ojiso, "don't you think that the high rate of divorce now has to do with the casual way that you young people choose your spouses these days?"

"How?"

"Young people of your generation often choose spouses casually and carelessly. You don't bring your relatives into the picture. All that matters is your own selfish judgment and satisfaction. So, if any difficulty develops in the marriage, there's nobody to mediate. The only thing left then is to rush into a divorce. Just like changing clothes. Divorce. Divorce. Divorce. A selfish solution that shifts the load from the spouses to the children. Easy come, easy go; that's the way today's youth see their spouse and marriage."

"It's a pity," Keli lamented.

"Yes it is. A bit less selfishness in choosing the spouse may reduce the tensions in marriage. And a bit less selfishness in rushing for the divorce option may reduce the hardship on the children."

"Yes. I know that there are situations where divorce is definitely called for," said Keli. "But it's a solution that must be used sparingly. Many people use it hastily to lift the burden from their heads, not caring that the burden now lands on the children. It's like a selfish quick fix."

"Anyway, I'm glad you're out there letting people know the evils of spousal abuse, and the importance of mutual respect in marriage."

"Yes," agreed Keli. "I talk about it often, formally and informally. Little did I know that I would be so directly challenged by this very scourge. Right in my own family."

"Strange, isn't it? Anyway, it's good that you have some official expertise on the matter. That should help us find a solution for Uju."

"Well, you know how it is," replied Keli. "It's easier to see the speck in somebody else's eye, than the one in your own eye. Anyway, we'll try."

Ojiso laughed, but not his usual guffaw, lest he should rouse the sleeping members of the household.

"So, what do you think?" Ojiso asked.

"My big concern is for those children that Uju left behind."

"Me, too."

"I think we should encourage Uju to return to her husband," suggested Keli.

"Yes, those children must be missing her very badly."

"She must return there. But we will lay down some very strict conditions for the husband."

"Like what?" asked Ojiso.

"We'll make it clear that if there's any further abuse, we'll reconsider the entire relationship."

Both Keli and his father knew that such a threat to Uju's husband was not new. It had been laid down on several previous occasions when there was strain in the marriage. What would be new this time was a mechanism for enforcing the stipulation.

"All those relatives of Uju's husband must face up to their responsibilities," continued Keli. "They must keep him on the straight and narrow. If he fails, they all fail; and we will not listen to them if they send another reconciliatory delegation to plead for him."

"I agree. They must realize that marriage in Alaku is a union between two families, not just two individuals. If the relatives don't play their supportive part, the marriage will not last."

"You'll have to speak very sternly to Uju's in-laws" Keli suggested.

"Don't worry. I know they're waiting for me to invite them for another peace meeting. I'll lay it all on the line then."

"Please do. I'm getting tired of all this nonsense."

"Me too," added Ojiso.

Again, there were a few moments of silence, while each one sifted through his mind to find the next topic. Ojiso was the first to find one, not that he had to look very far. It was always close to the surface as far as he was concerned.

"Now that we've decided what to do about Uju," Ojiso said, "let's move on to some developments around our family house here."

Keli waited for it.

"More precisely, concerning your plot of land," Ojiso continued. "As you know, too much delay is never a good thing. *Wa dọtịka ụta, nnụnụ efẹ.* Too much tugging at the bowstring to perfect the aim will only permit the target bird to fly off."

Keli adjusted himself on his seat, and braced himself for the usual barrage of arguments about why he needed to hurry up to erect a house in Alaku. But there was a new twist to deal with first.

"Two days ago, I heard that somebody has cut a trail through your designated plot," Ojiso pressed on.

"Oh my God!" Keli exclaimed, straightening up in his chair.

"The information I got was vague, but I've not had time to go and take a look. I suggest that as soon as we're done talking, you and I should go and inspect the plot."

Just then, Keli looked across the room. Approaching him in the semi-darkness was the ghost-like figure of Bedemu who had opted to pass the night with his grandfather in an adjoining room. He walked sleepily through the dim living room and found his place standing between Keli's knees. He was there for only a few seconds before moving over to Ojiso. The boy alternated listlessly from parent to grandparent and back again. In the somber eeriness of the dawning day, the ancestors looked down protectively on the three generations of their line, and marveled at the contrasting paths that destiny was carving for each of them. Like those ancestors, Ojiso was spending his entire life living in the traditional village. Unlike them, Bedemu was destined to spend all his life in the modernity of the city and the wider world. But what about Keli? He was a hybrid. He spent his early life in the village, but his adult life was being spent in the city. He had one foot in each place and was constantly torn between the demands of both places. The ancestors didn't quite know what to make of him.

A house here, a house there

Now that they were discussing the matter of houses and plots of land, Keli felt obliged to volunteer some information on his travails with respect to his house in Magotown. Partly because he knew that his father's priorities lay elsewhere, Keli was always sparing in what he told his father about his city house and the disastrous transactions surrounding it. Moreover, Ojiso's level of literacy made it superfluous to try to explain all the nuances of a modern-day real estate transaction. Keli usually told Ojiso only the barest outlines, while expecting full compassion, limited comprehension, and grudging resignation in return.

On this occasion though, Keli felt that he must let his father know one of the possible outcomes of his present travails: that he might indeed lose the house in the city. This was the very house to which he committed all his resources over the past many years; the house that was his ready excuse for lack of progress on his village house. After the brief pause caused by Bedemu's entry, Keli began his narration rather circuitously.

"You know you've always tried to provide for me," he ventured, addressing Ojiso.

"Yes?"

"That's exactly what I'm trying to do for my children," said Keli.

He raised his hand and gave a gentle pat on the head to Bedemu, who happened to be standing between his legs at the time.

"Yes, I want them to have a good future," Keli continued. "That's why I've been trying to secure that house that I bought in the city. I know you didn't like the idea, but I didn't do it for myself. I did it for them."

He patted Bedemu on the head again.

"Anyway, a slight problem has come up with respect to the house," Keli announced.

Ojiso straightened up in his chair.

"I have a hard time keeping up with the mortgage payments on the house. In fact, I now owe a huge sum on it."

"How much?" Ojiso asked.

"I don't know, but it's big."

"Chei!"

"However, an even bigger problem now is that the bank that lent me the money to buy the house is trying to take the house away from me."

Ojiso's brow arched upward, partly in surprise and partly in expectation of more details. But Keli was done. No more details were forthcoming. He ended his narration right there. He felt that there was no purpose served in bothering his father with the details of his troubles. He was particularly careful to avoid any mention of the visit to his city house by a flamboyant auctioneer who claimed that the house had already been sold to recoup Keli's indebtedness.

When Keli's long pause indicated that his information well had run dry, his father chimed in.

"Strange things happen in these modern times, especially in cities like Magotown."

"You're right, Baa," Keli agreed.

"Never in my sixty years of life have I seen a single person in Alaku lose his house to bankers, to creditors or to anybody else. Indeed, such a thing is alien to us and to village traditions. I'm sure that such things can only happen in the city."

"Yes. They do happen."

"That's why I've always favored building a house here rather than in the city. Do you think if you had built the house here, any stranger would dare to come to Alaku to take it from you?"

Ojiso paused, but wasn't really expecting an answer to his question. He continued. "Such a person would have to step over the dead bodies of all the youth of Alaku... It's just as if I knew."

Keli kept a humble silence.

"As our people say," continued Ojiso, "the touring dance troupe must ultimately return home. *Egwu techasia olue uno.* So I believe that you will someday find the means to build a house right here in Alaku."

Ojiso paused again for a few seconds.

"In any case," he continued ruefully, "I really feel sorry that despite all your struggles, things are not working out well with that city house. I know you're doing your best and using your best judgment."

Ojiso's gloom was palpable, and Keli quickly stepped in to minimize the damage.

"Don't worry, Baa. I have everything under control."

"Well, I know these must be very difficult times for you and your family. Try not to lose your composure. *Nwayo ka wa ji alacha ofe di okwu.* Soup that is piping hot has to be consumed with great caution."

Then, leaning forward towards Keli and Bedemu, Ojiso added pointedly, "Okolie, my son. Never forget your family background and upbringing. The honor of our family stands above everything else. *Ezi afa ka ego.* A good name is better than riches. We may not be rich, but we guard our honesty and honor jealously. I know the city is full of temptations. But your shield against all temptations is the armor of honesty. It's the armor that we've given you since you were a child. Stick to your high principles, and God will surely bless you. I pray that the spirits of our ancestors may bless you with peace and prosperity."

Keli thought of saying, "Amen," but held back. However, he was thrilled that the moral strength and anointing that he had traveled home to seek were now being delivered in full measure. Though he knew few of the details, Ojiso was now delivering moral and emotional fortification for Keli's on-going battles in the city. Father and son might differ in their opinions, but at the deeper level of feelings and emotions, they were inseparable.

As the discussion went on, the light of dawn was gradually winning the battle over the darkness of night. The rooster in the veranda had exhausted itself with repeated crowing. Sleeping household members in the various rooms got the message and were beginning to stir. It was a household made up of a curious mixture of nuclear family members and live-in relatives from the extended family.

Tradition dictated that on rising, each person had to seek out everyone who was older, to offer greetings. An adolescent boy, a live-in cousin to Keli, was the first to saunter into the living room.

"Baa, Okpa!" he greeted Ojiso, bowing slightly.

"*Ndo, nwam*," Ojiso replied. "*I teshi go?* [You've awakened?]" This was one of the ways that Enuani people said "good morning".

"Okpa, Baa," the boy repeated.

"*I lah
ukwa ọfuma?* [Did you sleep well?]" Ojiso inquired, using another variant of the "good morning" greeting.

"Ee. Okpa," was the positive reply.

But this boy was in a hurry. He terminated the iterative greeting sequence right there, as he rushed outside to urinate and bring relief to his overnight bladder. Other household members soon showed up to go through their own iterative greeting sequences. As in many Enuani situations, each greeting, once offered, triggered a series of back and forth iterative greetings that could drag on for a while. One by one, household members emerged from the shadows and commenced the greeting ritual, first with Ojiso, and then with Keli.

By the time four members of the extended household were awake, Keli and Ojiso could no longer carry on their discussion without interruption. The interruptions were becoming frequent. Father and son found it difficult to concentrate. Moreover, the walls, which were deaf at the start of their meeting, had grown ears. With so many ears now alert, the confidential atmosphere needed for serious family discussions was lost. There was no motion for adjournment, but neither discussant needed any prompting that it was time to wind up the meeting.

It's your land, so what?

With the pre-dawn meeting over, Keli and Ojiso left to inspect Keli's plot of land. Bedemu, curious as ever, tagged along. With Ojiso holding his walking stick and leading the way, they took the winding path that ran eastward from the family house. A few yards down the path, Ojiso stopped abruptly. He swung around to face the other two. Then he said, "This is where I transplanted some orange seedlings two days ago."

He pointed his walking stick to a spot beside the path. Without waiting for a response from the other two, he walked some four paces to a spot off the path.

"Here they are," he said, pointing. "I'm glad they're doing fine."

"Yes, I can see," said Keli.

"They're for your children."

"My children?"

"Yes. In keeping Alaku tradition, I nurtured the three orange saplings as my gift to your three children."

"Bedemu, one of them is yours," Ojiso continued.

"Thank you, Baa!" exclaimed Bedemu. "That one in the middle is the tallest. I'm claiming that one."

"That's fine, my son. You're the oldest of the children anyway," Ojiso said.

"Thank you very much," Bedemu enthused. "I promise to nurture it till it produces some large juicy oranges."

"Good, my boy," exclaimed Keli.

The trio continued on their walk along the path. The initial pace was casual, not even enough to break a sweat. As the winding path took them past the house of their neighbor, Okocha, they shouted out greetings to the awakening family. There was no response, but at least they had registered their presence, as a signal that they were passing through. As they picked up their walking pace, they had to stop twice to let the trailing and distracted

Bedemu catch up. Bedemu could just barely keep up because he stopped after every few steps to engage with any insect or flower that he happened upon. His child-like curiosity was being fed a feast of exciting novelties.

In ten minutes, they were at the plot. Keli had not visited the plot in many, many months, and had trouble recognizing the site. It was virtually a piece of bush. Successive generations of weeds had germinated, flourished, flowered, and re-seeded on the plot since Keli's last visit. Perennial climbers and shrubs boasted thick stems and branches, with birds nesting on some of the denser clumps of shrubbery. Even the heaps of mason's sand and gravel that Keli deposited months earlier could just barely be discerned in the thicket. What was not difficult to discern was a freshly-cut trail that ran diagonally across the dormant plot. The trail went a few yards beyond Keli's plot, and then stopped at a trap for wild animals. The trap actually lay outside the plot, but the trail was the pathway through which the prospector walked to inspect his snare.

"This must be the intrusion that they told you about," said Keli, thoroughly alarmed.

"Yes. It seems that somebody has been setting traps for bush meat around here," Ojiso said in a light casual manner. "I hope he succeeds."

"Whose trap do you think it is?" asked Keli anxiously.

"I don't know. But it must be one of our relatives."

"Relatives or not, why didn't they seek permission from you before going in here? They all know that you're the custodian of this plot while I'm away in the city."

"What permission?" asked Ojiso.

"Permission to enter."

"Why?"

"They must have known that it's our property."

"Yes, they know. Do you see them building a house on it?"

"But what about the trail? That's how encroachment usually starts."

"What encroachment?"

"So you don't think he means any harm?" asked Keli, still unsure of his father's stance.

"This is nothing, my son. When I got the report that something was going on here, I didn't know how serious. Now I see it's just somebody looking for bush meat. I hope he catches what he's after."

"But do we know who it is?"

"Why do you want to know?"

"I want to know so I can keep an eye on him, and perhaps even give him a stern warning to keep away."

"They'll just laugh at you. Everybody will laugh at you. In Alaku, a path like this is no trespass. You see, it's customary for villagers to enter designated plots in order to try to make a living. They may be searching for wild game, laying traps for animals, collecting mushrooms, fetching firewood, or looking for snails. When you own a piece of land here, it doesn't mean that others cannot use it. *Ụla emebinẹ anya.* Sleep does not damage the eyes, even though eyes are for seeing."

"How?" interjected Keli.

"They can use the plot, so long as such use does not interfere with the intended use of the primary owner. As you know, the land belongs to all the people."

"Yes," added Keli. "It seems we're all joint owners of Alaku land."

"Correct."

"And that must be why the village gave me this plot free of charge to start with."

"You're right," Ojiso confirmed. "All that I offered the village on your behalf was just a calabash of palm wine and some kolanuts. Nobody asked for a penny for the plot they gave you. Not one penny."

"In Magotown, one would pay a huge sum of money for land like this. And over there in the city, ownership is ownership. Rights to a plot of land are exclusive and absolute. No subsidiary uses by others are permitted."

"Even if the primary owner of the plot has no immediate use for it?"

"Yes."

"You city folks are strange," said Ojiso, shrugging his shoulders.

"Even the mere act of walking through a designated plot is considered as trespassing. Large tracts of land lie idle, fenced off by their rich purchasers. The most that ordinary city folk can do is to cast envious glances at the vacant plots. Trespass, even in the form of physically walking through, is strictly prohibited and severely punished."

"That's a very greedy system you city people have. Here in the village, you take what you need, and leave the rest for others. Don't worry, whoever cut the path through your plot means no harm."

"I still would like to know who did it," said Keli.

"If you really want to know, I can find out. But truly, it doesn't matter."

Standing in front of his plot, Keli could not help but feel the sheer weight of the construction burden that lay before him. A burden whose gravity was being multiplied by the downright distasteful developments surrounding his house in Magotown. For now, at any rate, he was relieved that his rights to the Alaku plot had not been infringed. No substantive trespassing had occurred on his plot.

On their way back to their house, the trio stopped over at the house of Okocha, the neighbor whom they had hailed on their way to the plot. Okocha and his household were now awake. Blue cloudy smoke oozing lazily from his kitchen area indicated that his wife's morning chores were well under way. When Keli's group arrived, Okocha was hunched over a slab of stone in front of his house, feverishly sharpening his machete in preparation for a brief foray into the bush. He quickly dashed into the recesses of his house and came out with a long bench which he offered to the visitors to sit on. But only Ojiso sat down. Keli was obliged to remain standing, in deference to the fact that Okocha, his senior in age, was not seated. Bedemu found his usual place, nestled between Ojiso's bent knees. His entire attention was devoted to exploring a moth that he had picked up along the path.

This was the most casual of visits, but Okocha still thought it necessary to apologize that he had no kolanuts to offer to his visitors as a sign of welcome. Meanwhile, he continued sharpening his machete in fits and starts, as they all chatted in the warming rays of the rising sun.

"You both are up early," said Okocha, grinning.

"Sure," replied Ojiso.

"And was it not you that called out to me about half an hour ago? I was just rounding off my sleep then."

"But you usually wake up early to get some farm work done before the hot sun shows up," replied Ojiso. "I expected you would have left the house by now."

"Yes, today is an exception. I went to bed very late. That's why I've let the sun get up before me." Okocha grinned again; this time, broadly enough to reveal his full array of tobacco-stained front teeth. He indulged regularly in snuff and chewing tobacco. He hadn't yet partaken of some tobacco that morning, but the stains from years of indulgence were clearly in evidence.

Then turning to Keli, Okocha added, "You city people never get up early like we do here."

"But then," replied Keli, "we never go to bed as early as you do here in the village. We often joke in the city that village people are like domestic fowl. They go to bed as soon as the sun goes down."

"You know we don't have electricity, which turns your night into day," Ojiso chimed in. "So, as soon as the sun goes to sleep, we follow its example and go to sleep, too. We do what nature says. We don't have things like night clubs and television to distract us."

"So, how are things going generally in the city," asked Okocha, testing the keenness of the machete blade on a banana leaf.

"Well, we're managing," replied Keli.

"What about your wife Dada, and the other children?"

"They're doing fine."

The conversation was going well enough, but Ojiso was keen to ferret out some specific information about Keli's plot. So, he changed the topic slightly.

"We've just been to Keli's plot over there."

"I'm glad he's still maintaining an interest in it," said Okocha. "I'm sure one of these days, he'll surprise us with a mighty mansion on that plot of land."

"Yes. We went to take a look. It's so very bushy," said Keli.

"Sure. Bushes grow very fast during the kind of rainy season we've had this year," volunteered Okocha.

"I noticed that somebody has been setting traps near that plot," said Ojiso.

"You mean traps for bush meat?" asked Okocha.

"Yes."

"I saw my son cutting a path through there two days ago. You know he's a very keen hunter. He likes prospecting for wild game. I try to encourage him to do his own thing, especially now that he's almost a man. I hope he didn't damage anything on the plot."

"No. Not at all. And we wish him luck," replied Ojiso.

"He never catches anything big. But I think the exercise and practice are good for him."

"So where's he now?" asked Ojiso.

"He's not yet come home from last night's hunt. But he should be here shortly."

"Greet him for me when he returns. Tell him that we wish him the best of luck," Ojiso concluded.

The information needed had been gleaned. Keli's anxiety was soothed. The trail, and the trap to which it led, represented no attempt to take over the plot. This was normal practice. No harm was intended, no foul committed. No feelings were hurt, no apologies needed.

Fun Festival or Fetish Feast

Early morning was no time for idle chit-chat in the village. It was a period to mobilize for the day's farm work or other chores. So, Ojiso was soon on his feet and they were bidding goodbye to Okocha. As they were leaving, Okocha reminded them that the traditional *Ozizi* festival would take place at the village square later that day. Bedemu, who had not heard about *Ozizi* before, jumped up in excitement as he coaxed his grandfather into promising to take him to the festival. Bedemu did not have to try too hard. There and then, he extracted a promise from Ojiso that he would take him to the festival.

Ozizi was the second most sacred festival among the practitioners of the traditional religion in Alaku. It involved animal sacrifice, prayers to the spirits of the ancestors, and worship of the *Ikenga* idol. In the eyes of some people, it involved plain unadulterated idolatry. Ojiso was a keen practitioner of this religion, as was his father before him. There was no clear-cut priesthood in the religion, but Ojiso was as close to one as you could get. He performed all the rituals, and was always present when other persons or the community performed theirs. He had an important role in the ceremonies coming up that afternoon, but Bedemu would tag along simply to enjoy the fun and traditional dancing that accompanied the ceremonies. Ojiso was fully aware of the upcoming festival. He needed no reminding.

Keli, on the other hand, needed reminding. More than that, he needed prodding. True, he attended *Ozizi* festivals for several years in early childhood. But all that was before he enrolled in the village primary school run by Christian missionaries. He encountered Christianity at school, embraced it, and retained it as he worked his way through secondary school and university. He became a staunch Christian, albeit a first generation one. Marriage to Dada, an equally staunch Christian, gave considerable reinforcement to his religious beliefs and practices. To him, much of what went on in the traditional religious practice was idolatry, pure and simple. As a Christian, he would have no part of it. And this included the *Ozizi* ceremonies. Like the name Okolie, *Ozizi* for him was a relic of the past for which there was little room in his modern lifestyle.

When they got back to the family house, the trio brought out chairs and sat briefly under the mango tree in the front yard. The cool of the morning was worth every bit of the peace that Keli was seeking.

"I always look forward to *Ozizi* every year," Ojiso said. "It's the highlight of the season for me."

"Yes. I must go with you today," said Bedemu. "Will there be dancing?"

"Sure. It's all very exciting," said Ojiso. Then turning to Keli he asked, "You'll surely come along to *Ozizi* this time, won't you?"

"I doubt it," Keli replied.

"I suspected as much. I've failed in all my previous efforts to convince you to attend *Ozizi*. You say it's against your religion. Anyway, I thought I should try once again to persuade you. You don't know how much you're missing."

"It doesn't matter. I hope you and Bedemu enjoy it. That's good enough for me."

"I knew I couldn't convince you. But Okolie, remember our people's saying, that he that declines food is maltreating his own stomach. *Ọjụ nni mejọ afọ a,*" Ojiso concluded, shrugging his shoulders.

Having given up on Keli, Ojiso became restless on another score. His village instincts told him that this was valuable time when villagers typically attended to important chores. His palm wine needed collecting from the tree, and his traps needed to be inspected in case they had snared any bush meat overnight. So, after a few more minutes, Ojiso excused himself, leaving Keli and Bedemu to continue enjoying the village peace under the mango tree.

Keli's mind roamed all over the place, from one imponderable problem to another. But Bedemu was focused on his moth, and on the prospects of an exciting time at *Ozizi*. In his child-like way, he was curious as to why his father was willing to pass up such an exciting opportunity. He voiced his feelings.

"Daddy! I think you should come with us to *Ozizi*. Baa says it will be very exciting."

"Sorry, my child. I just can't go," Keli replied.

"I heard Baa say that you consider *Ozizi* to be against your religion. Is that true?"

"Yes. It's a bit true."

"But it's not against Baa's religion?"

"Yes. We have different religions."

"But doesn't the difference affect your relationship?"

"Not really. You see, each of us tolerates the differences, and we respect each other. He doesn't try to convert me, and I don't try to convert him. Occasionally, I even support him in his religion, and he supports me in mine."

"How?"

"Take last Easter for example. You remember that on Easter day, Baa went to church with us. Similarly, I sometimes provide him money for his *Ikenga* worship and ceremonies."

"So, do your two religions have anything in common?" inquired Bedemu.

"They have many things in common."

"Like what?"

"Let me give you one example. Let's take honesty. Even though the two religions seem different, each of them emphasizes morality, honesty, and respect for human beings. Even before I reached school age, Baa had already taught me these principles, which he derived from his traditional religion. It's true that his religion has animal sacrifice, ancestor worship, *Ikenga* worship, and things like that. But traditional religion was the source of the high moral standards that Baa taught me as a child."

"So what happened when you started going to school?"

"You know that our primary school here in Alaku was established and run by the Christian missionaries. So, once I started schooling, they began to teach me about Christianity, and I embraced it. Baa allowed them to baptize me, even though he refused baptism for himself. But do you know something? I found that Christianity taught the same moral principles that Baa had taught me. There was no conflict."

"No conflict?"

"None," replied Keli. "None at all. There was tolerance instead. So, I was able to build upon what I had learned at home. With such similarities, religion is not a factor in my relationship with Baa. We get along very well."

"So, if I decide to take another religion when I grow up, you won't be opposed."

"Not at all. I think your mother and I have already laid the moral foundation for you. Any other religion that you embrace will only be building on our foundation."

"Alright. I'll tell you all about *Ozizi* when we come back."

"Enjoy it, my son. I'll be waiting to hear your stories."

After a few more minutes, a relative from the family house called out to Bedemu to come for breakfast. He hopped off to the house, leaving Keli alone under the mango tree, to continue his restless rumination. At his abode in his cousin's house, Keli's breakfast had already been delivered, piping hot. It was there, getting cold by the minute. Keli had more pressing things to think about. The doves that normally patronized this mango tree seemed to have vanished, replaced by hawks and vultures. Contrary to his hopes, the weekend visit only succeeded in padding his portfolio of problems. The spiny burdens of Mr. Atlas had not diminished. And they managed to pierce through the bucolic peace of Alaku.

☼ Chapter 3

The Bat Hangs Upside Down:
Metaphor For The Enuani Condition

"Do me I do you, God no go vex"

So you think you've got enemies? Wait till you hear about the enmity between Iwegbu and Nwafor. And between their wives. And between their children. And between their extended families. This brand of enmity was bitter. Bitingly bitter. Bitter like *onugbu* bitterleaf. Bitter like *ẹdu* bitter-kola. Bitter like quinine medicine. Bitter to the bone like the cold harmattan wind of the dry season. And like the harmattan, this enmity inflicted its dry dusty chill on every facet of life in Anibaba, their little rural town. Cold hatred was the flammable fuel for the burning fire of hot enmity.

To worsen matters, each person that was born into the enmity was expected to propagate it dutifully, without questioning. And they did. Thus, the enmity was able to remain strong from generation to generation. Over the years, many people in Anibaba tried to mediate, but to no avail. Some mediators simply had their mediation efforts rebuffed. They were the lucky ones. Other mediators, for their pains, got their names added to the list of enemies by both camps. Most people were now resigned to simply watch the situation, and hope that time would heal matters.

The enmity had its roots in distant ancestry. Its original cause was no longer clear to anybody alive. Some say it originated when the oracle determined that Iwegbu's grandfather was the source of the poison that caused Nwafor's grandfather to be paralyzed in the left leg. Others say it had to do with land matters. But the actual cause was no longer relevant. All that mattered now was that the enmity existed, and that members of each family dutifully maintained it through time.

Occasionally, peace overtures would come about, and the fervent hope would sprout that the enmity would finally be buried. Hope would spring eternal, and everybody would agree that it was time to repair the fractured family relationships. Then, just as occasionally, an unpleasant brush between the two families would cause some of the bitterest aspects of the enmity to rise to the surface. Exactly such an occasion had recently forced itself to everybody's attention. Anibaba was being shaken by one of the resurgences of enmity between the two families. Iwegbu and Nwafor were the two opposing members. Their paths had crossed. And like two electrified wires coming in contact, sparks were flying.

The latest crisis started innocently enough. For the second time in a month, Nwafor's free-ranging goat had gained access to Iwegbu's backyard farm and wreaked devastating damage to the yams and cassava. The cassava stands were left leaning at all kinds of crazy angles, with most of the leaves eaten off. The yam tubers were forcibly yanked from their rope anchors on the barn, and eaten. Those not fully consumed lay strewn all over the barn area as nondescript half-eaten pieces. To add insult to injury, the goat did considerable damage to the fence that Iwegbu had painstakingly constructed to protect the barn. Months of hard work at the farm were rendered meaningless by the goat's ferocious foray.

When the encroachment by the same goat first occurred, Iwegbu was not aware of the ownership of the goat. He captured the goat alright, but was content to bear his loss, release the goat, and hope that the incident would not recur. In any case, the damage then was minor and was quite easy to bear.

On this second encroachment, Iwegbu again caught the goat red-handed. He was infuriated by the repetition of the intrusion, and by the more extensive damage done by the goat this time. Then, to his chagrin, a neighbor identified to him that the goat belonged to none other than Nwafor. Nwafor, his bitter enemy. Nwafor, his congenital nemesis. Now, the whole episode took on a new dimension and new meaning. Maybe the goat was not straying after all. Maybe it was on a deliberate mission from Nwafor to destroy Iwegbu's means of livelihood. Maybe the goat was bewitched. Maybe it was sent to convey a bad omen to Iwegbu's extended family. Maybe.... The diabolical possibilities were endless.

If this goat belonged to anybody else, Iwegbu would have sent a very stern warning to the owner to tether his goat; and that would have been all for now. After all, free-roaming goats in Anibaba did damage to property all the time. But a goat from Nwafor's family? Possibly on a diabolical mission? Surely it had to die, if only to neutralize and dispel the evil spirits which it embodied.

Iwegbu meticulously tied up the arrested goat, bringing all four legs together so that it couldn't move. He then laid it on its side and sprinkled some wood ash over it, in an elaborate attempt at bestial exorcism. Next, he produced a piece of native chalk *(nzu)* from behind the water pot in his room. He held the chalk in his right hand over the goat. Then crushing the chalk, he let the crushed powder descend in a cloud over the immobilized goat. All this while, Iwegbu was reciting incantations presumably appropriate for the exorcism in progress. He invoked his ancestors, asking them to bless him for his willingness to fight their enemies. He promised that just like them, he would never give up on the fight.

Then without further ado, Iwegbu slit the goat's throat and let it die. The death sentence had been pronounced and carried out. The spell which the goat embodied would surely die with its body.

Iwegbu did not feel squeamish about slitting a goat's throat. After all, this was an act that he performed every few months as part of the sacrifice to his *Ikenga* religious idol. *Ikenga* demanded animal sacrifice, and Iwegbu obliged as often as he could. Most heads of household in Anibaba did the same. The only difference was that this time, Nwafor's goat was being sacrificed at the altar of enmity.

As soon as bleeding stopped, Iwegbu stuffed the dead goat in a disused bag, and conveyed it to the market square. There he deposited it. As a *coup de grace,* or perhaps as a souvenir, Iwegbu cut off the goat's tail and kept it with him as he returned gleefully to his home. Then, he sent word to Nwafor that his goat lay dead at the market square, awaiting collection. This was a tantalizing taunt, targeted at his arch enemy.

Nwafor could not believe his ears. He was sure that his goat showed no signs of sickness. A sudden death could only mean one thing: that it had been killed. And with the message coming from Iwegbu of all people, Nwafor suspected the worst. Suspicions were confirmed when he overheard some women, returning from the stream, chatting innocently about a dead goat at the market square. They mentioned that its throat had been slit, and some wondered why the butcher that slit the throat did not complete his butchering task.

Nwafor immediately convinced himself that Iwegbu was complicit in the foul play that killed his goat. The tradition in Anibaba was that owners of free-roaming livestock received a warning if their animal went on a rampage. Nwafor felt that he at least deserved a warning from anyone whose property may have been trespassed by his goat. This time, there was no warning. No admonition. No caution. And for Iwegbu to be the one notifying him about the goat? When did goodwill start flowing his way from Iwegbu and his family? Surely, nothing good could come from Iwegbu. Iwegbu must be up to something.

To make matters worse, this particular goat did not even belong completely to Nwafor. His brother-in-law had an interest in it. The goat was given to Nwafor by his wife's brother to "keep" in the traditional sense, as a way of strengthening family bonds. In this practice, the understanding was that offspring from the goat would be shared between donor and keeper. Now, what was Nwafor to tell his brother-in-law?

The loss of the goat was one matter. Bad enough. But the humiliation which Iwegbu was orchestrating for Nwafor in the episode was quite another matter. By depositing the dead goat at the market square, and perhaps forcing Nwafor to collect it from there, Iwegbu intended to inflict the maximum amount of humiliation on his life-long enemy.

For Nwafor, collecting the dead goat from the market square was totally out of the question. Sure, a freshly-killed goat could fetch a handsome price, especially at the hands of proprietors of pepper-soup joints. But how could he, Nwafor Isieche, be seen to be bullied and defeated by his mortal enemy. How could he allow himself to become the laughing stock of all of Anibaba? What would his own kindred say if he disgraced them by collecting the dead goat? Would weakness on his part not anger the spirits of his ancestors, and trigger retribution from them? He, therefore, resolved to ignore Iwegbu's message concerning the goat. At least he pretended to ignore it.

Before long, repercussions started. Casual passers-by at the market square noticed the dead goat lying there. One well-meaning villager in mid-afternoon, totally innocent of the circumstances, rushed to Nwafor's house to inform him that his goat was lying apparently dead at the market square. Nwafor thanked the messenger, and dismissed him, pretending that he had not earlier been informed. But he remained unshaken in his resolve not to attempt to retrieve the dead goat.

As evening wore on, the early stages of decay set in. The carcass grew louder in its demand for attention from any passer-by within smelling distance. The houseflies and blowflies, ubiquitous enough in Anibaba, now seemed to have found a home on the carcass. They greeted each passer-by by noisily dispersing for a while, before again re-convening to finish their fetid feast.

From the time in mid-morning when he received the message from Iwegbu, Nwafor confined himself to his house. This was mainly to enable him to nurse his anger quietly, and to deliberate on what line of action to take. It was also partly an attempt to avoid being confronted by other villagers who might have noticed that his dead goat was at the market square.

Shame on you, shame on me

The people of Anibaba did not fail to note the fact that the dead goat remained unclaimed at the market square by night-fall. Everyone was certain that if the goat had died of natural causes, the owners would have retrieved it within a couple of hours. Such owners would try to cut their losses by either selling the carcass, or processing it for their own domestic consumption. Such was the value of meat in Anibaba that even a goat that died of unknown causes was considered fair game. So why, the villagers wondered, why was this particular dead goat being allowed to fester and go to waste in the market square? Surely, there was something to it; and everyone waited with baited breath for whatever it was to unravel.

Uti, Nwafor's friend living near the market square, also saw the dead goat. He recognized it as belonging to Nwafor. With instincts honed by many years of living in Anibaba, he suspected that something was amiss. He decided to go to Nwafor after nightfall to find out.

Before it was completely dark, Uti arrived at Nwafor's home. Nwafor had just concluded his supper, and was sitting in the patio, brooding over the events of the day. Soon, kolanuts were presented as a sign of welcome. The kolanuts were broken with a brief incantation of blessings. After the sharing of the kolanuts, Uti felt free to broach the topic of his mission. There was no time to waste. He started obliquely.

"You know, you and I have been friends for a long time," Uti said.

"Yes. Since our childhood," Nwafor replied.

"You help me when I'm down, and I help you when you're down. As our people say, *Aka nni kwọa aka ekpe, aka ekpe akwọa aka nni.* The right hand washes the left, and the left hand washes the right."

"So it is."

Uti took a bite from his remaining kolanut. Then he lunged into the matter at hand.

"There's a black goat I used to see around here," he ventured, not quite sure of Nwafor's frame of mind. "You told me your brother-in-law gave it to you to keep."

Nwafor nodded.

"Where's the goat now?" Uti inquired.

Nwafor stared blankly at the floor for a while. Then looking up at Uti, he said, "*Daalu*, my dear friend. Thank you. Indeed, I was just thinking of coming to your house to discuss the issue of that goat. But thank God, you've taken the initiative to come here first."

Uti nodded, then leaned forward a bit more.

"I know that many men in Anibaba have seen that goat lying in the market square," Nwafor continued. "But you're the only one who has seriously come to ask me about it. I thank you greatly."

"You know I always have your interest at heart."

There was a brief pause as Nwafor tried to gather his thoughts.

"You know how it is between us and Iwegbu," Nwafor continued. "I mean between my kindred and his kindred."

"Everybody in Anibaba knows."

"Now, Iwegbu is trying to provoke me with insults."

"How?"

"You saw my goat lying at the market square. That was Iwegbu's doing."

"Are you sure?"

"Sure? I can swear by my ancestors. And he had the daring to send me a message to come and collect it. No warning. No caution. He just killed my goat like that."

"Sorry. *Ndo.*"

"And he wants to humiliate me on top of that. Who does he think he is? Stupid man. He's playing with fire, and I'll burn him back."

At this point in the discussion, Nwafor was practically shouting, giving vent to the rage that welled up within him. He was like a devil possessed. Once or twice, Uti intervened by reaching out with his hand to try to calm Nwafor down.

When Nwafor's fiery ire subsided a bit, Uti himself assumed a pensive mood. Sure, he suspected that all was not well when he set out to visit Nwafor. But he did not prepare himself for this depth of feeling. Or this height of passion. He knew how even the simplest matter assumed grave proportions, once it involved Nwafor's and Iwegbu's families. The devil himself could not have manufactured a graver scenario for trouble, than for Nwafor's goat to invade Iwegbu's farm. Trouble was brewing. Knowing that the enmity between the two families was severe, Uti was not confident that this present eruption would lend itself to easy resolution.

After ruminating for a couple of minutes, Uti consoled Nwafor for what happened.

"It's a pity things have come this far," he said. "But my advice to you is to take things easy. The sages say that an eye for an eye will only result in everybody going blind. This matter should be handled with utmost care. As our people say, *Odudu be-do n'akpa amụ akọ ka wa ji egbu ẹ.* One must exercise great caution when trying to kill a tsetse fly that is perched on the scrotum. Nobody wants a remedy that is more damaging than the ailment."

A pregnant pause followed. Then Uti asked, "So, what do you intend to do now?"

Nwafor's anger again exploded.

"I'm going to burn his house. I must answer fire with fire!"

Uti was alarmed. Such rampaging rage could not be allowed to run loose. It was like a venomous vermin, primed and poised to do damage. It had to be corralled and contained. Otherwise, a lot of havoc and harm could come to all of Anibaba before the expected cycle of retaliation ran its course.

Uti did his best to calm Nwafor down. He lectured him extensively on the nature of traditional law and jurisprudence.

"You know that by Anibaba custom, everybody keeps goats, pigs, sheep, and chicken, all of which roam freely," Uti said.

"Yes. That's our way of life."

"Normally, you're not blamed for the actions of your free-roaming livestock."

"Just like mine."

"Sure. But owners of livestock that prove too destructive usually receive a warning. This gives them time to take appropriate action."

"Exactly," concurred Nwafor.

"They could tether such livestock, confine them, slaughter them, or sell them off."

"That's what people do."

"Even if your goat trespassed Iwegbu's property, it seems that Iwegbu acted rashly. It seems that he was driven by the longstanding enmity between your two families."

"How dare he!" Nwafor shouted.

"Yes. It appears that he provoked you. But my advice is this. Rather than take the law into your hands and retaliating as Iwegbu has done, you should seek redress by reporting the matter to *Onotu*."

Let's try the traditional justice system

Onotu was the traditional peace-keeping council in many communities among the Enuani ethnic group. And the town of Anibaba was no exception. Onotu passed judgement in serious matters likely to cause a breach of the peace. It routinely handled such matters as the deliberate destruction of somebody else's farm, livestock, tree crops or bush traps. Before Western influence came, even such grave matters as murder were within the jurisdiction of Onotu. They thus maintained peace and justice within the community, and did so effectively for centuries before the advent of Western-style police and courts. Even in modern times, Onotu has continued to be useful as a council of first recourse, settling innumerable civil disagreements that might otherwise threaten the peace of the community. More serious criminal matters, inevitably, get referred to the police and regular courts.

Nwafor was thoroughly skeptical about Uti's suggestion that he should take the matter to Onotu.

"I've taken many things to Onotu before," he said. "And none of the verdicts was even half way satisfactory."

"But I think you should give them one more chance. This time, things may be different."

"I doubt it. Do you know something? I suspect that members of Onotu have become tainted with the modern-day disease of bribery. Bribery. That is what has spoilt the police and the courts which the white man brought us as his modern judicial system."

"Don't even mention the police," Uti suggested.

"Onotu of old was incorruptible. Each member swore before the town's strongest idol that he would uphold justice and fair play. They believed firmly in the idol, and they believed in the oath."

"Oh, yes."

"Any temptation towards injustice was immediately resisted out of fear of the idol."

Indeed, the expected retribution from the all-seeing, unforgiving, idol was enough to keep Onotu members honest in times gone by. It was of little relevance to ask if the idol indeed had such powers. All that mattered was the fact that everybody believed that the idol had such powers. And this belief had the desired restraining effect on those charged with the administration of traditional justice.

"And do you know what has happened in modern times?" Nwafor continued.

"Tell me."

"In modern times, Onotu has become tainted. It's now a ghost of what it was in earlier times."

"How?" asked Uti.

"For one thing, the coming of Western religion has seriously eroded belief in the traditional idol. To the point where most Onotu members are not serious when they take their oath before the idol. They just go through the motions. They do not seriously believe in the power of the idol, and they fear no immediate punishment if they fail to adhere to the oath."

"It's really a pity."

"They don't feel compelled to keep the oath. They just feel free to do as they wish. Some even decline to take the oath at all."

Truly, belief in the idol was no longer widespread. Gone was the one binding force which earlier compelled a fair dispensation of traditional justice. The new situation permitted malpractices to creep into Onotu. Nwafor was sure of that. Otherwise, how could anyone explain the recent spate of grossly perverted verdicts coming out of Onotu?

"No. I will not take this matter to Onotu," Nwafor declared with a tone of finality.

But Uti would not take no for an answer, fearing what might happen if Nwafor was allowed to run loose along the course of revenge. Uti enlisted all his persuasive powers, hoping to wear Nwafor down by sheer force of argument and persistence.

In the end, Uti's efforts began to pay off. Nwafor began to give ground. Sensing an opening, Uti sought to sweeten the pill. He offered to accompany Nwafor when Nwafor would go to lodge the case with Okuche, the leader (chairman) of Onotu.

"I'll escort you to Okuche to lodge your complaint," Uti offered.

"Thank you."

"I'll even provide the required palm wine that we'll take to Okuche. You just bring along the kolanuts. As you know, you can't go on such a mission without kolanuts and palm wine."

"Thanks, my dear friend…. When do you think we should go to Okuche?"

"This matter is very serious," replied Uti. "We better not let it sleep around for long. How about going at dawn tomorrow morning?"

"Fine. We'll get there before Okuche departs for the farm."

"Agreed. I'll come to your house here and we'll proceed together."

At the conclusion of the visit, Nwafor escorted Uti for a few yards beyond his compound. They then parted and Uti picked his way home cautiously through the village darkness.

Nwafor had a sleepless night. In his wakefulness, all he could hear was the haunting hooting of several owls in his backyard. And all he could think about was the flagrant insult from Iwegbu. He was chafing in anger at the humiliation that Iwegbu was packaging for him. A publicly-visible form of revenge was his first choice in terms of action. That way, his battered honor and family dignity would be restored, and all of Anibaba would know better than to mess with him and his kindred. However, having given his word to Uti, he felt obliged to give Onotu a try. With luck, he might achieve his objectives within the existing traditional legal framework.

Uti was faithfully punctual the following morning. He arrived at Nwafor's residence at about 5 a.m., toting a small calabash that was frothing effervescently with palm wine. Nwafor got dressed, picked up the packet of kolanuts, and the party was on its way to Okuche's house. Incidentally, their route took them by the market square. It was still fairly dark, so Nwafor was spared the sight of his decomposing goat. But the unmistakable stench that greeted them as they passed near the spot was enough proof that the contentious carcass was still there.

They arrived at Okuche's house just as he was waking up. Another man, with his own case to lodge, was already waiting for Okuche when Nwafor and Uti got there. Okuche appeared briefly in the living room where the visitors were waiting. He disappeared for a few minutes to rinse his face and mouth, before rejoining the visitors.

Okuche signaled to Uti and Nwafor to step outside so the other man could lodge his case confidentially. They stepped outside, but could overhear what the matter was about. Apparently, somebody deliberately destroyed a set of traps which the man constructed in the bush. He now wanted to lodge the case with Onotu.

When the man was done and ready to depart, Okuche signaled to Nwafor that it was his turn.

As per custom, Nwafor first presented the kolanuts and the palm wine. One of the kolanuts was picked out, placed in a wooden saucer and held up to Okuche. The kolanut was blessed, broken, shared. Next, it was time for libations. A small amount of the palm wine was poured in a cup and given to Okuche. He pronounced the requisite incantations to the ancestors while methodically dribbling some drops of the wine onto the floor. He then gave the rest of the wine in the cup to Nwafor to drink, since he was the presenter. To guard against possible poisoning, it was customary in Anibaba for the presenter of a drink to sample it first.

Introductory rituals over, Nwafor could now address the business at hand. He narrated in summary, his allegations against Iwegbu. Okuche took mental note of the submission, and promised to summon the full Onotu shortly to consider the case.

***

Within one traditional market "week" (four days), Iwegbu had been notified of the case lodged against him. The members of Onotu had also been informed. The meeting to handle the case was scheduled to hold in two traditional market weeks.

By the third day after it was deposited there, the goat carcass at the market square had become considerably distended. Its rapid deterioration was accelerated by a slight drizzle on the second day, and by the warm humid weather. Before daybreak on the fourth day, putrefaction had reached the stage of physical disintegration. The reproductive activity of the flies was becoming obvious, as writhing wriggling maggots made an eyesore of the scene. By this time, most people in Anibaba had heard the story behind the abandoned goat carcass. Perhaps because of this, nobody dared to remove or even go near the decomposing carcass. The air hung thick with stench, gossip, and expectation.

By the fifth day, the goat carcass was gone. It was no longer there. Only the fetid stench and moist effluent on the spot gave any clue as to what had been there before. Was the carcass dragged away and destroyed by Iwegbu in an attempt to erase the evidence? No. Did Nwafor claim it, as Iwegbu desired? No. Instead, some stray dogs happened upon it at night. Having had their fill, they apparently dragged off the remaining portion to an unknown location. They cared little for the compunctions of morality, legality, and hygiene that prevented humans from tampering with the carcass all these days.

Onotu assembled shortly after dawn on the appointed day. It was an Eke market day when many Anibaba villagers rested from farm work. Nwafor was in attendance, dutifully escorted by Uti, his faithful friend. Iwegbu was there too. The two litigants were seated at opposite ends of Okuche's living room. Everybody else exchanged greetings with one another and with the litigants. But neither Nwafor nor Iwegbu could find it within himself to spare a greeting for the other. The best they could offer each other was a prolonged petrifying glower.

Iwegbu came with his case well prepared. Too well prepared, some might say. In the four days preceding the meeting, he paid at least one nocturnal visit to each of the five Onotu members. Each visit was consummated with various presents, ranging from lengths of smoking tobacco, to bottles of *esimesi* (native gin) plus, inevitably, a parcel of kolanuts. Okuche received two such visits. The second visit occurred on the day before the Onotu meeting. On that second visit, Iwegbu's motley array of gifts was upgraded to include a large bottle of imported whiskey. During the visit to each Onotu member, Iwegbu did his best to convince his host of his innocence; that Nwafor was acting out of malice and enmity; that if anything, Nwafor should be punished for trying to implicate Iwegbu and wasting the time of Onotu.

Nwafor, by contrast, made no deliberate effort to visit the homes of Onotu members. Even when he chanced upon one of them on the farm trail three days before the meeting, they only reminded each other of the date of the meeting. There was no attempt to persuade, or even to discuss the details of the case. This was nothing compared with the deliberate blitz by Iwegbu to prepare and poison the collective mind of Onotu.

The gathered Onotu meeting sat down for the serious business of dispensing justice. Kolanuts were broken and shared amidst casual banter about how the farming season was progressing. After introductory remarks by Okuche, Nwafor was asked to state his case against Iwegbu.

Nwafor narrated all that had happened, going over more meticulously this time, the details that he covered when he came to lodge the case with Okuche. All Onotu members listened attentively, without comment. When Nwafor finished, he leaned over to Uti who was sitting beside him.

"Can you think of anything I missed?" he whispered to Uti.

"Nothing. I think you said it all," Uti replied, with a vigorous series of nods.

Nwafor sat down, exuding an aura of satisfaction.

Iwegbu was now called upon to refute the charges against him. Iwegbu got up, cleared his throat, adjusted his loin cloth, took a deep breath, and was ready to begin. He exuded confidence far out of proportion to what was expected of a defendant in a serious case. He greeted Onotu members one by one, each by his own specific traditional greeting. Then, with pompous airs like a Roman orator, he felt his way towards his tale.

"You all know what our people say about the millipede," Iwegbu began.

Some of the listeners nodded.

"*Esu wa zọ ụkwụ akwana ákwá, mana onye zọa nị asị na ụya egbue yẹ*. When the bare-foot pedestrian steps on a millipede, the injured millipede says nothing. But the pedestrian who has inflicted the harm shouts and screams and bemoans his fate at having stepped on the millipede."

Iwegbu paused for a moment to let the full import of his parable sink in. Onotu members looked on, most nodding. Iwegbu continued.

"The party that inflicts the injury is angry, while the injured party licks his wounds quietly. So it is, with Nwafor. Is it not clear to everybody that Nwafor is the aggressor, and I the victim? Yet, is it not the same aggressor that is now fuming and taking offence against me, the victim? He's even going to the extent of lodging this case before Onotu and wasting our time, while weeds take over our farms."

Iwegbu paused to allow Onotu to absorb his opening salvo.

"Look at him over there in the corner," Iwegbu continued, pointing at Nwafor. "Nwafor, the perpetual troublemaker in Anibaba. Nwafor, the owl that only hunts at night. Nwafor, the producer of tiny yams who, instead, celebrates his manhood with cocoyam. Nwafor, the creepy crawling crab that's always moving sideways, never forward. Nwafor, the sneaking snake that has no bite. What a pitiful figure! Look at him!"

Iwegbu's diatribe and counter-charges against Nwafor ran on for over fifteen minutes. It was long on exhortation and emotional appeal to Onotu members, but very short on details of the events that led to the crisis. What detail there was, consisted of a curious mixture of truth and falsehood. Yes, a goat of unknown ownership had twice invaded his backyard garden. The damage done was more than the price of a goat. Yes, on the second occasion he caught the goat, tied it up, and delivered it bleating and kicking to the market square so that whoever owned it could collect it. He knew nothing about the slashing of the goat's throat, or the message to Nwafor to come and collect the dead goat at the market square. His (Iwegbu's) second wife whom Nwafor claimed to have delivered the message was currently away on a trip; otherwise she would have come to testify that there never was such a message.

In the end, Iwegbu's presentation distilled itself down to two points. First, Nwafor and his goat were the aggressors and offenders. Nwafor should therefore be fined for bringing such a frivolous case before Onotu. Second, Iwegbu was the injured party, and should receive substantial punitive damages from Nwafor to make up for his losses.

At the end of his elaborate oration, Iwegbu sat down, brimming with all the confidence and satisfaction of a lawyer who felt that his case had been clinched. For good measure, he scowled once again at Nwafor, partly as a sign of derisive disregard, and partly to ascertain whether his masterful oration had inflicted the desired damage on Nwafor's morale.

Following normal practice, Okuche now asked Onotu members if they had any questions for the litigants. There was silence, but eventually one member spoke up.

"*Ikpe ahagaa onwe ẹ nụ*. The verdict has delivered itself," he said.

"Yes," agreed another. "Let's hurry up. The sun is rising rapidly in the sky."

"Are you going to the farm on this Eke day?" inquired a third.

"No," replied the second. "But I have to inspect my traps and run several errands. Let's save time."

"Yes. There's no need wasting more time," concluded the first.

Since there were no questions or further comment, Okuche asked Nwafor and Iwegbu to step outside, to permit Onotu to discuss the case. Uti, too, was obliged to leave the room.

Discussion was intended to be brief. Perhaps reflecting the diligent homework which Iwegbu had done on them, Onotu members were virtually unanimous in their verdict: Iwegbu was not guilty. Okuche was perfectly happy with this verdict and was willing to leave the matter there. But some of the more hawkish members pressed on. It was not just that Iwegbu was not guilty; he was the victim of provocation and loss through Nwafor's negligence. He needed to be made whole. They argued that in addition to losing his case before Onotu, Nwafor was the guilty party and had to be fined. Okuche was not comfortable with this aspect of the verdict, and said so. But he was effectively overwhelmed by the number and vigor of the other members. One extreme partisan even proposed that Nwafor should be fined twice: one to be paid to Onotu for wasting its time, and the other to be paid to Iwegbu as compensation.

Okuche could not overrule the militants, nor could he let them have their way by putting the matter to a vote. Both overruling and voting were not normal processes of decision-making in Anibaba. Instead, most decisions were arrived at by consensus, a process that invariably required more time and discussion, but which had the eventual advantage of preserving the solidarity of the group. So, the discussion on the verdict dragged on much longer than was expected, while the litigants waited anxiously outside.

It was an unpleasant wait for the litigants outside. Iwegbu was bent on inflicting the maximum humiliation on Nwafor. He vigorously paced back and forth in front of where Nwafor stood, spitefully spitting in Nwafor's direction a couple of times. Nwafor offered no resistance, and pinned his hope for satisfaction on the expected verdict.

When the dust settled, the litigants were invited back into the room. Okuche pronounced the consensus verdict. Iwegbu, the original defendant, was exonerated and commended for his restraint. Nwafor, the plaintiff, was pronounced guilty and fined forty tubers of yam, payable to the town.

Justice had been perverted, and Nwafor knew it. Onotu let him down disastrously, once again. He simply could not believe his ears when he heard the verdict. He knew something fishy happened, but as yet, he was unaware of the extent to which Iwegbu went to influence the verdict. At any rate, the verdict justified his loss of confidence in Onotu, as well as his initial reluctance to refer the case to it.

Uti, on whose insistence Nwafor went to Onotu, now felt badly betrayed. His own confidence in this traditional council of settlement was severely shaken. As he trailed haplessly behind the fuming Nwafor on their way home from the meeting, he could not help being gripped by a certain sense of foreboding. If Onotu could no longer be trusted to dispense justice and reconcile disputants in Anibaba, then the traditional peace-keeping machinery was in decay. There was nothing to prevent people from taking the law into their own hands.

I'll do it my way

Nwafor hurried to pay his fine. He did so more out of spite than out of a willingness to comply. Within a week, he delivered the required yams to Okuche. He wanted to acquit himself of all present and future ties with Onotu. Having paid his fine, he considered himself free to carry on his future life as if Onotu did not exist.

Freed from the shackles of reliance on a corrupt Onotu, Nwafor busied himself contemplating how best to administer his own justice. His humiliation and material losses at the hands of Iwegbu inflamed his passions. His only thought now was on how best to exact revenge. He did not wish to discuss the matter with anyone. Not even with Uti, who, at any rate, became reluctant to exert any restraining influence on Nwafor after the Onotu fiasco. Many diabolical options presented themselves to Nwafor. For the next couple of weeks, his mind was the devil's workshop, something normally associated with idle minds. But his mind was not idle. It was busy concocting callous calamity.

On Thursday, Nkwọ market day, about twenty-three days after the infamous Onotu meeting, Anibaba was astir. Iwegbu's main yam barn was up in flames. This was his major barn, located about a mile from the village, and much larger than the backyard barn which Nwafor's goat had invaded.

The fire started from a clump of dried grass near the stretch where the communal farm path ran past Iwegbu's *ugbo-ukwu* (main farm). That was where the fire started, but nobody knew how. By the time late returnees from the farms noticed the fire, Iwegbu's entire barn had been engulfed. The bamboos making up the framework of the barn were crackling and exploding furiously in the heat, while the stench of burning yam rent the air in all directions. An alarm was raised, and people responded from the village. They flailed and beat around fruitlessly. They deployed twigs, sand, buckets of water, and even cutlasses, all in an attempt to contain the fire. In the end, the fire was contained, but not before it had devastated Iwegbu's yams and barn, along with a neighboring cassava plot. The only reward for all the fire-fighting effort was that the fire did not spread to all the other village farms nearby.

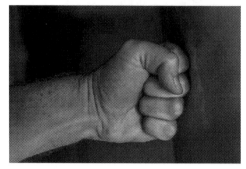 Iwegbu was out of town on the day of the fire. He had gone to Abuja two days before the fire, and was not due back for several days. In the circumstance, Iwegbu's relatives picked up the gauntlet and tried to ascertain the cause of the fire. Suspicion soon fell on Nwafor.

Within a few days, rumor went round Anibaba that Nwafor had burned Iwegbu's barn. Nwafor himself, more by design than by accident, did very little to deflect the suspicion. He confirmed to inquirers that he passed by the burned area earlier that day on his way to his own farm. He confirmed that he passed there again on his way back, barely twenty minutes before somebody else raised the fire alarm. He confirmed that as a smoker, he had both his pipe and matches in his possession as he went to and from farm on that day. But to the ultimate question as to whether he did indeed set the fire, Nwafor declined to give any answer, positive or negative. He simply kept silent, and in the end, each inquirer was left to draw his or her own conclusions. Most drew the conclusion that the fire had been deliberately set. And that Nwafor was the perpetrator.

Iwegbu returned from his trip four days after the fire. His relatives briefed him immediately about the incident, their investigations, and the obvious conclusions. He agreed entirely with the conclusions. Since his resounding victory at Onotu, his mood had been jolly to say the least. But this fire incident changed all that. He was now overcome by a mixture of gloom and rage, as he contemplated another round of confrontations with Nwafor and Nwafor's kindred.

Iwegbu also contemplated the sheer symbolism of what Nwafor did. To any man of Anibaba, the yam harvest, stored in the barn, was the ultimate symbol of his manhood and productivity. He might produce a million tons of cassava, maize, cocoyams, or other crops. But if his yam harvest was un-presentable, so was his manhood, and he was considered a failure. This explained why the yam, to the virtual exclusion of all other crops in the area, had so many festivals and even a god associated with it. Not only was there a new yam festival, but yam was the one crop that featured prominently in traditional gift-giving, fines and rituals. The yam was the man; and the destruction of Iwegbu's yam harvest was tantamount to an assault on his manhood. Much honor stood to be lost if the assault was not demonstrably and decisively repulsed.

Any inclination to faintheartedness on the part of Iwegbu was effectively repressed in the face of the war-like mood of his relatives who met him on his return. They were drawn so deeply into the matter by the sheer accident of Iwegbu's absence. But having initially carried the mantle, they were now in no mood to let go. The general demand was for action. Swift action. And Iwegbu knew that he had no choice but to oblige them.

Action, yes. But of what sort? Was he, Iwegbu, now to go ahead and burn Nwafor's yam barn? Or perhaps his house? Or perhaps his rubber plantation? The options were many, and were not totally confined to arson. But then, there was a problem. Having won his case so resoundingly at Onotu, Iwegbu had gathered a considerable aura of respectability around himself as a law-abiding citizen. Furthermore, his recent trip outside Anibaba was in connection with the prospects of his being appointed groundskeeper at the government health center which was due to open shortly in Anibaba. Any rash action on his part at this time would certainly damage his prospects for the job, and erode his hard-earned reputation as a law-abiding citizen.

So, against his best instincts, Iwegbu decided to seek redress through the legal and para-legal channels available in Anibaba. And where else was a case of destroying somebody else's yam barn to go except, inevitably, to Onotu? For the second time in as many months, Iwegbu would appear before Onotu. Last time as the defendant, he succeeded in getting the plaintiff fined. Now as the plaintiff, who knows what goodies lay in store for him?

Within a week after his return, Iwegbu went to Okuche to lodge his case, with kolanuts and palm wine as dictated by custom. Two days later, both Iwegbu and Nwafor were informed that the case would be heard two traditional market weeks (eight days) from then. This was enough time perhaps for Iwegbu to make his nocturnal rounds to Onotu members once again.

But Iwegbu elected to play it differently this time. He figured that the effects of his previous round of visits might not have completely worn off. So, he spared himself the effort of visiting each Onotu member personally. He simply sent his son with a parcel of kolanuts to each one of them, reminding each one that he would see them at the meeting in a few days. Actually, Iwegbu would have been content not to bother contacting any Onotu members prior to the meeting. But he had the lingering suspicion that Nwafor, having learned the lesson from him, might now be busy trying to buy the minds and consciences of Onotu members. Iwegbu felt that he needed to neutralize any such move by Nwafor.

Iwegbu could well have spared himself the effort. Why? Because Nwafor, too, elected to play it differently this time. He had other plans.

By sunrise on the appointed day, Onotu was in full session. Every member that was expected to be there, was there. Even the fragile Okolie, long bed-ridden, somehow managed to put up presence at this Onotu meeting. It was his first meeting attendance in four months. Iwegbu was there, accompanied by his cousin and farm neighbor whose cassava plot was burned in the infamous fire. The room was overflowing with people and brimming with anticipation.

Kolanuts were produced, broken with elaborate ritual, and distributed with meticulous attention to hierarchy. Everyone now expected the proceedings to commence. This was the only case to be heard at this meeting, and everyone hoped that it could be handled quickly enough to permit a full day's work at the farm afterwards. But there was a problem. Nwafor had not yet arrived.

To pass the time while they waited, Onotu members traded jokes and stories about happenings within and outside the town: the forthcoming opening of the health center; the high cost of farm inputs; the best way to preserve kolanuts; why postal workers were on strike; the perennial scourge of dust during the harmattan season. All the while, everyone kept a healthy distance from events that might be even remotely linked with the fire incident which was now *sub judice.* For his part, Iwegbu sat at a safe physical distance in one corner of the room, contributing occasionally to the jokes, but being careful not to appear to be fraternizing too much with his potential judges.

Twenty minutes after the kolanuts were broken, there was still no sign of Nwafor. Thirty minutes. Thirty-five. The group was becoming restive. The repertoire of jokes and stories was beginning to run low. Irritation was setting in, not only at the delay *per se,* but also at the prospect that the day's farm work might have to be forfeited.

Onotu's sense of time was jarred into consciousness when the first bell tolled at the school yard to summon children to school. This bell always tolled at 7.15 a.m. Still no sign of Nwafor. The group agreed to send for Nwafor. Okuche's third child, all washed and dressed up for school, was pressed into service to go and call Nwafor. The boy scurried off, rushing not to be late for school. He was in Nwafor's compound in a matter of minutes.

"*Daalụ nụ o!*" he exclaimed as he approached the shut front door.

He knocked on the door twice and waited for a response. There was silence.

"*Daalụ nụ o!*" he repeated, louder this time. "Is anybody home?"

He pounded on the door several more times. There was still no response.

The boy soon returned to Onotu with the inevitable message. Nwafor was not at home, and there was nobody at his home.

One of the younger Onotu members offered to repeat the errand, not convinced that the boy had discharged the errand correctly, or that he had knocked hard enough on Nwafor's door. He went to Nwafor's house, then pounded persistently at the front door for about three minutes. With no response forthcoming, he went round to the backyard, but was only greeted by an empty silence. Having failed in his assignment, he returned dejectedly to Okuche's house, where he briefed the gathering about his abortive mission.

Without the defendant, the case could not proceed. Onotu, having run out of options, dispersed. Most members left rather hurriedly, trying to catch up on the day's farm work. So, there was little time for them to discuss Nwafor's absence, or to ponder its significance. Only the thoughtful Okuche began immediately to explore the depths of his experienced mind to try to fathom the reasons for, and the meaning of, Nwafor's failure to show up. His mind threw up each possibility, weighed it, and dismissed it. But he could not help fearing that the absence might have been intended as a deliberate snub on Onotu.

Of all the persons that attended the abortive Onotu meeting, Iwegbu was the most disappointed that it did not hold. He had spent long periods in the preceding days rehearsing his presentation, while at the same time deflecting pressure from his militant relatives for more direct retaliation. Now that the meeting was postponed, what was he to do? Should he give up on Onotu and yield to the pressure of the militants? At any rate, it was clear that he would have to endure several more days of unrelenting pressure and unrequited loss.

Before sundown on the day of the abortive Onotu meeting, Nwafor was at Okuche's house, looking penitent. He explained, with a large measure of falsehood, how he had travelled to Onitsha on the day before the meeting, hoping to return in the evening. How the vehicle which was bringing him back in the dead of night broke down. How it proved impossible for him to find alternative transportation; how he was obliged to spend the night at the road junction; how he finally made it back to Anibaba by motor-cycle taxi several hours after the scheduled Onotu meeting; how he deserved to be pitied for his pains and suffering. The story went on and on.

Okuche listened attentively. He was hugely relieved to see Nwafor. The details and truthfulness of his narration were of secondary importance. It was enough for Okuche that Nwafor did not, after all, absent himself on purpose. He did not intend to snub Onotu. Otherwise, he would not have come so quickly to explain his absence from the morning meeting.

Okuche's relief was premature. True, Nwafor was out of town on the day preceding the meeting, and at the time of the meeting itself. But he went nowhere near Onitsha. All the story about the vehicle breaking down and his sleeping at the road junction, were mere cock-and-bull concoctions. Since the day Onotu handed down the outrageous verdict against him in the case of the slain goat, Nwafor had made up his mind never to appear before Onotu again, whether as plaintiff or as defendant. So, when the summons came for the case relating to the burnt barn, he did not for one moment entertain the possibility of honoring it. Yet, he feared the possible consequences of a blatant and open defiance of Onotu. A head-on collision might be too disastrous. A slightly more tangential approach seemed better. So, he decided to use trickery in effecting his refusal to appear. The day before the case, he traveled to visit his mother's relatives in the next rural town, only five miles away. There, he stayed until noon the following day, before returning to Anibaba and going to Okuche's house. His pretended remorsefulness was only a ruse, intended to divert the immediate anger of Onotu. The plan was to let Onotu be introduced in a graduated fashion to his prepared path of rebellion and defiance.

Okuche took Nwafor's narration at face value. He hoped it was true, and took it as such. But when he later narrated it to other Onotu members, some of them were clearly skeptical and suspicious. However, all resolved to give the benefit of doubt, and to try to fix the case for another date. They were not in any particular hurry.

But Iwegbu was in a hurry. Chafing under the weight of the uncertainty, he wanted the matter to come up again very soon. In his usual manner, he put pressure on both Okuche and Onotu members in order to have his way. Before long, Okuche fixed a date. Onotu members, Iwegbu and Nwafor were all duly notified. As usual, the meeting would start just before sunrise.

Very early on the appointed day, Nwafor left for his farm, along with his wife and children, leaving his compound in the silent custody of roaming chicken. Onotu assembled at the appointed time. Onotu, again, waited. This time, they did not bother to send any emissary to try to fetch Nwafor. Having exhausted their patience, they permitted Iwegbu to address them.

It did not take much, or long, for Iwegbu to convince Onotu that Nwafor was guilty, and was only employing delaying tactics to frustrate the course of justice. A substantial fine was imposed on Nwafor. This time, the fine included compensation for Iwegbu for his burned yams, in addition to money payment to be made to the village purse.

On this occasion, Nwafor did not bother to go to Okuche's house later in the day to tender any fake apologies. He did not really care anymore whether or not Onotu members were able to detect the meaning and significance of his absence. That was their business, not his.

Any lingering doubts about Nwafor's intent were soon dispelled. Unlike the previous instance, Nwafor failed to pay his fine on time. A week passed; two weeks; a month; two months; and Nwafor was yet to react to Onotu's latest verdict.

***

For Iwegbu, Nwafor's delay in paying the fine proved extremely frustrating. He received neither the material compensation for his losses, nor the social redemption of his honor which would occur when Anibaba saw that Nwafor had been forced to pay a fine. And having gone to Onotu and obtained a verdict, the option of direct retaliation on Nwafor, so much championed by Iwegbu's relatives, was no longer available.

What added to Iwegbu's frustration was that Nwafor's daily activities in the town were in no way curtailed, confined, or constrained by the verdict against him and his failure to pay the fine. Nwafor moved around freely. He attended various social functions and communal events without let or hindrance. He was just as accepted and as acceptable as he was before he embarked on his defiance of Onotu. For all practical purposes, there were no social consequences to his rebellion.

Matters came to a head ten weeks after the imposition of the fine. As was customary, Nwafor sought permission from the village chiefs to celebrate his annual personal *ịlọ mmọ* festival, a high point on the calendar for each practitioner of the traditional religion. Despite Nwafor's rebellion, the traditional authorities in the village did not withhold permission. Nor did they insist that the fine be paid before the festival could proceed. Ostracizing Nwafor for his defiance was the farthest thing from their minds. Instead, the festival went ahead and was attended by the cream of Anibaba society, including virtually all the Onotu members. There they were, eating, drinking, and fraternizing with the rebellious Nwafor. Such was the pervasive hypocrisy in Anibaba. So, apart from the fact that the verdict and fine had been pronounced, nothing, absolutely nothing, changed. Nwafor, of course, was perfectly happy with this situation. But it was driving Iwegbu to distraction. He was like a pressure cooker, ready to explode at any time.

Four months after the unredeemed verdict was pronounced, Iwegbu summoned up courage to go to Okuche to complain. This one was a late evening visit, after supper.

"Welcome, my brother," Okuche said, as he concluded the kolanut-breaking ritual.

"Thank you," Iwegbu replied. "You've probably had a hard day working at the farm."

"Yes. The weeds are growing faster than my crops. So, I had to do a lot of weeding today. Very tedious work."

"With you being so tired, I'm lucky to catch you before your bedtime."

"Yes. We often go to bed early during this peak of the farming season."

"I won't keep you up much longer…. It's about Onotu."

"What about it?"

"You remember the last time I came to Onotu?"

"Yes. And you got a very handsome verdict in your favor."

"It's about the verdict."

"What?"

"Since that verdict, nothing has happened. Nwafor has not paid any fine. I haven't got my compensation. And the fine for the village purse hasn't been paid either."

"It seems so."

"Well. Can't you see that Nwafor is spitting on Onotu? Ignoring it and farting on it?"

"I hope not," said Okuche.

"He's making you look foolish. And he's making me look foolish for seeking justice at Onotu. To worsen matters, do you know what?"

"What?"

"Your Onotu members are helping Nwafor to spit on all of us."

"How?" asked Okuche.

"Did you not see all of them at Nwafor's *ilọ mmọ* festival, eating and drinking with him? He's owing the village a huge fine and he should be treated as an outcast. Shame on him. And shame on all of Onotu," Iwegbu concluded, his voice rising to match his passion.

Okuche was surprised at the venom in Iwegbu's language and the emotion in his voice. After a few moments of tense silence, Okuche spoke.

"But you know that there's nothing I can do."

"There's plenty you can do," Iwegbu exploded. "You can ask the town to ostracize Nwafor. And Onotu members can start by doing so themselves."

"Easier said than done."

"Why?" asked Iwegbu.

"As you know, I can't control the lives of Onotu members. I don't have the power to ostracize anybody. Neither does Onotu."

"Somebody must have such powers," Iwegbu suggested.

"The *Obi* (king of Anibaba) has been duly informed of Nwafor's stubbornness. He has the power to ostracize. But the Obi is taking his time on the matter. It just happens that he's Nwafor's cousin. He might be in no hurry to take any action."

"You know I'm a law-abiding citizen, and a strong supporter of Onotu," Iwegbu stated.

"That I know."

"Now, if Onotu should become only a bulldog without teeth, I will stop supporting them. I will stop bringing any cases to Onotu. There are other options, you know."

Okuche stared at Iwegbu in disbelief. Then he leaned over to him and said pointedly, "I have done my best. What more do you want me to do with Nwafor? Do you want me to poison him?"

The questions were rhetorical, of course. But Iwegbu clearly got the message that Onotu had reached the limits of its power. The traditional system of justice lay before him like a disused rag. In tatters.

Iwegbu left Okuche's house with his confidence in Onotu hanging by the thinnest of threads. Onotu's ability to provide him needed redress was now clearly in question. True, it served him well in the past. With very little material inducement, the members always returned the verdicts he desired. But now, it appeared that the partnership had run its course. The limits of Onotu power were staring Iwegbu in the face. His confidence in it was oozing. He might have to strike out on his own to seek justice outside the workings of Onotu. Unlike Nwafor who deserted Onotu because he saw it as corruptible and corrupt, Iwegbu was deserting Onotu because it appeared powerless. The effect was the same. Each of them felt free to try to secure redress, retaliation, or retribution by whatever alternative means they could devise. Other options were looking attractive.

I'll go one up on you

A little over two months after the barn fire incident, the post of groundskeeper for the health center was filled. Despite his strenuous efforts and expense, Iwegbu could only come second at the interview to fill the only vacancy available. The top-scorer accepted the job, and was set to start work. No prospect there for Iwegbu.

The disappointment of not getting the job added to Iwegbu's frustrations. But curiously, it released him from the need to continue to wear his new-found garb of respectability. One of the factors that restrained him from taking direct revenge on Nwafor was now removed.

 Then a couple of months later, the remaining restraint was removed when Iwegbu finally lost faith in Onotu. He was now a free man. All his thoughts became focused on direct revenge. His relatives, who had all along advocated direct retaliation, were only too happy to welcome Iwegbu to their line of thinking. They laid their plans, tuned and re-tuned their strategies, and waited for the appropriate opportunity for implementation.

***

Early one Friday morning, Anibaba woke up to the dreadful news that there was a dead body lying beside the road near the school compound. Early-rising school children, on their way to sweep the classrooms, scurried back on beholding the frightening sight. Women heading to the forest to fetch firewood detoured through alternative paths in order to avoid the spot.

As daylight came, the inevitable truth dawned on Anibaba. Nwafor lay dead near the school. He had left home the night before on one of his occasional nocturnal visits to his concubine living across town. His wife had, over time, come to accept his habit of sometimes spending the night at his concubine's place. So, on this occasion, there was no alarm when he failed to return home before bedtime. But Nwafor had, indeed, intended to return. He was on his way back when tragedy struck. Unknown assailants, perhaps three or four in number, ambushed him and, after a vicious exchange, stabbed him fatally.

The assailants did not remain unknown for long. Nor apparently did they wish to remain so. At about 8 a.m., while Anibaba was still in a state of paralyzed inaction, three men showed up. They looked officious and businesslike; so, every onlooker gave them a wide berth. They went straight to the corpse, and with utter contempt and disregard, dragged it the fifty or so yards to the edge of the market square. This they did in full view of the assembled horde of curious school children, their teachers, and a few villagers. Having deposited the body near the market, each of the three men spat on it in turn. Then they sat down a few yards away and started to chat as if nothing had happened. After a few minutes, one of them went behind the ceremonial iroko tree nearby. Most observers thought that he went there to relieve himself. But plumes of smoke soon began wafting from behind the tree, suggesting that the fellow was sneaking a smoke of something unusual. He emerged after about seven minutes, swaggering and hailing the other two as he walked towards them.

Ikpeze, one of the school teachers who watched this display, did not know what to make of it. He knew each of the three men to be natives of Anibaba. Indeed, he recognized them as members of Idumu-uya kindred. They even muttered something about redeeming the honor of Idumu-uya. This was the very kindred to which Iwegbu belonged. But Iwegbu was not one of the men.

Ikpeze walked over towards the three men. From a safe distance, he suggested that it might be best to call the police. He was surprised at the reply he received.

"Nobody," one of them snarled back, "Nobody should dare to call the police into this matter. If you do, you will regret it. We'll handle this matter ourselves!"

Ikpeze couldn't believe what he was hearing and seeing. From what they said and the way they were carrying on, he was convinced that these men were out of their minds. He could even perceive the strong odor of marijuana wafting from their direction.

He felt thoroughly scandalized by what he saw going on, more so since his pupils were watching. His sense of patriotism just could not permit him to stand by and watch the abominable scene that was unfolding before him. He decided to rush to the Obi's palace to seek consultation on whether or not the police should be invited.

Ikpeze met the Obi in a pensive mood. One of his advisers was seated before him, offering a mixture of condolence, consolation and advice. The Obi already heard that Nwafor was murdered. But he was as yet unaware of the activities of the three young men at the market square. Ikpeze supplied that detail, and elaborated on the sordid complexion which the whole murder episode was acquiring. Any previous wavering on the Obi's part immediately fell away. He knew that from time immemorial, the maintenance of law and order within Anibaba was the ultimate responsibility of the Obi. He was still the final arbiter in minor disagreements within the town. But since the advent of Western authority with its police and courts, serious breaches were inevitably referred to these authorities to handle, albeit with the Obi's consent. And how serious a breach could you have than an apparent case of brazen, undisguised, murder?

Ikpeze further told the Obi about the supposed murderers' threat to deal harshly with anyone who invited the police. This last detail, ironically, went to confirm the Obi in his resolve that this case was clearly beyond him. The Obi pleaded with Ikpeze to go on his motor-cycle to lodge a complaint at the police station which had jurisdiction over Anibaba. The station was located nine miles away, two towns away.

Ikpeze yielded to the Obi's entreaties. But first, he needed to go to the school to seek permission from the headmaster for his absence. As Ikpeze passed by the market square on his way to the school, he could see that the young men were still there, gloating over their kill. They were apparently undecided as to what next they should do. The dead body was still there too. The only difference was that it had now been stripped to the waist, and the risen sun was gleaming balefully on Nwafor's exposed torso. Ikpeze hurried past without a word. But before he was completely out of ear-shot, one of the young men noticed him and shouted, "If we see police here, you will join this beast lying here!"

"We've warned you," concurred his colleague, just emerging from behind the iroko tree.

Ikpeze dutifully got his clearance at the school. He collected his motor-cycle from home, and rode off to the police station, taking a side road so as not to pass through the market square.

The reception Ikpeze got at the police station was less than encouraging. The officer on duty complained that there were only two of them at the station at that time, and as such, there was no one to accompany Ikpeze to Anibaba. Of the complement of staff nominally assigned to the station, one officer was on leave, one went to testify in court at Kwale, one was ill, and two went to Umunede to pursue an investigation. If, as expected, the latter two returned in early afternoon, then someone would be available to answer the call at Anibaba. Ikpeze was given a sheet of paper to write down his report. Then he was told to go home and await the arrival of the police.

But before Ikpeze left, the officer made one final point: the police could only answer the call at Anibaba if transportation was provided. The station vehicle, if one could call it that, lay in decrepit bits and pieces all over the station compound, and had been so for over two years. Nor were there funds in the station budget to cater for travel. All traveling by the policemen had to be done by taxi or by volunteered transportation. The travel expense was borne by complainants or whoever felt that they needed the police presence most at that particular time. This practice, of course, had peculiar inequitable consequences for the distribution of police protection within the area. Those who were unwilling or unable to afford the cost of police transportation simply had to do without the services of the police.

Ikpeze pondered his options. One option, suggested by the officer, was for him to come back at noon and convey one, or possibly two, policemen to Anibaba on his motor-cycle. This option was not attractive to him. Not so much because of the wear and tear it would inflict on his machine, nor because of the wastage of time entailed. Instead, the unattractiveness stemmed from the fact that Anibaba people generally resented the idea of anybody bringing policemen to the town. To be so physically involved in conveying policemen to Anibaba on this occasion would surely earn Ikpeze the general displeasure of Anibaba as a whole. Not to mention the ire of the three men at the market square. Such general disapproval would not necessarily arise if he simply made a report to the police, and left them to make their own way to Anibaba.

The second option for Ikpeze was to simply return home and inform the Obi that he had made his report, and then feel absolved of responsibility if the police should fail to show up. But this line of action would totally negate the patriotic zeal that drove him to get involved in the matter in the first place. Moreover, the Obi might just turn around and send him back to the station to convey the police.

So, Ikpeze's mind moved on to consider one more option. The offer of money to the police for transportation was common practice in the area, but Ikpeze reserved it as the last option to be considered. Though nominally for transportation, such offers were usually several times the expected cost of the trip. The greater the excess money, the greater the expected level of cooperation or favoritism from the police. Indeed, the offer of "transportation money" had become an accepted euphemism for offering bribes to the police. Ikpeze's brief did not include offering any money to the police, for transportation or otherwise. So, any offer he would make would be strictly on his own initiative and from his own purse, with little hope of reimbursement back home.

Reluctantly, very reluctantly, Ikpeze parted with money, meant as "transportation money". It probably came closer to the truth, closer to the actual expected fare, than most offers made for the purpose. This fact made Ikpeze a bit apprehensive that the sum might be rejected as being too small. But just as reluctantly as the offer was made, the officer accepted the offer, promising to "try my best".

His unpleasant mission seemingly accomplished, Ikpeze returned home and reported back to the Obi. He made no mention of the transportation money, for fear of appearing too mean. Anibaba waited with baited breath.

No. Let's try the modern justice system

At half past noon, a taxi stopped on the road opposite the Obi's palace. Two policemen alighted. They went straight into conclave with the Obi, who dutifully narrated all he knew about the incident. He ended by informing the policemen that their task was simplified because of the three young men who so openly identified themselves with the murder all morning long.

When the policemen got to the market square, the three young men had vanished. The dead body was still there, but the three men, who constituted its guard of dishonor all morning long, were nowhere to be found. There was a small crowd of sympathetic villagers, but most kept their distance from the body for fear of being implicated. The police would have loved to speak with the three presumed murderers, and, if possible, arrest them gently. But now that they had vanished, there was the distinct possibility of a lengthy search and violent resistance. This was nothing that this detachment of two policemen from the station could confront by itself. Reinforcements were clearly needed. Moreover, there was the need to make arrangements to remove the dead body for police autopsy.

The policemen decided that one of them would return to the station to radio for reinforcements and a police ambulance from the divisional headquarters. The other policeman would stay behind in Anibaba, to collect more information on the incident.

At ten minutes past five in the evening, while it was still light, a police Land Rover and an ambulance breezed into Anibaba. The Land Rover conveyed six policemen, armed to varying degrees. They drove straight to the body at the market square. Photographs were taken. The body was then loaded onto the ambulance which sped off dustily, leaving a troubled Anibaba behind.

The Land Rover and its occupants paid a brief call on the Obi, and then settled down to the serious business of trying to round up the suspected murderers. They went to the house of one of the young men who menaced the corpse all morning. They surrounded the house, guns on the ready, commando style. Then their leader tapped on the door.

The police could well have spared themselves all the armament. The man who answered the door was precisely the man they were looking for. He surrendered without resistance, and in a few moments, was safely in handcuffs, inside the Land Rover. The pattern repeated itself at the homes of the other two young men. So, in less than an hour, the police mission was accomplished. All three suspects were securely under arrest.

In their briefing, the police did not fail to note the antagonistic relationship between the deceased and Iwegbu. Nor did they think that it was a coincidence that all three arrested persons were from Idumu-uya, Iwegbu's kindred. It was only logical, therefore, that having arrested the three young men, they went to Iwegbu's house to try to arrest him, or at least to haul him in for questioning. Iwegbu was not at home. Nobody seemed to have set eyes on him all day, despite the bizarre events that were unfolding in Anibaba, and the prominent role being played by his relatives. Iwegbu was in hiding.

The truth of the matter was that Iwegbu and his three relations had hatched a plot to teach Nwafor a lesson. Nwafor was to be waylaid and given a thorough beating. But that was all. He was to be let go after the beating so he could return to his home. The three young men had clearly exceeded their brief. Nobody asked them to stab Nwafor; nobody asked them to kill Nwafor; and surely, nobody asked them to glory in their gory deed all morning long. The execution of the plan had gone haywire. The executors of the plan became executioners. Worse still, they saw their deed as a badge of honor that restored the damaged pride of Idumu-uya. How else could one explain their keenness to be identified with the deed, and their willingness to be arrested by police? They probably saw themselves as martyrs for the cause.

Iwegbu was now afraid because of his complicity in the whole affair. He rightly believed that in the present charged atmosphere, nobody would care to make the fine distinction between commissioning a beating and commissioning a killing. He obeyed his best instincts and decided, at least for now, to go into hiding.

Having failed to find Iwegbu, the police contented themselves with arresting his second wife who was at home. They later released her when Iwegbu's younger brother volunteered to go instead.

With their vehicle brimming with their catch, the policemen returned to the divisional headquarters. Their joy came mostly from the fact that their mission had gone reasonably well. No resistance and no bloodshed. But there was also gleeful anticipation that gladdened their hearts. Each suspect that they apprehended represented an opportunity to make illegal money through extortion. The officers and their bosses knew how to play the dirty game.

***

The normal reaction to an arrest in Anibaba was for the members of the kindred to rally round. Such rallying was without prejudice to the presumed guilt or innocence of the arrested person. Nor was it much related to his popularity or social standing within the group. To be away from home in police custody was always seen as an abnormal situation which had to be rectified. Ironically, the rallying intensity diminished drastically if the individual was allowed to return home on bail, or if, at the other extreme, he was convicted and imprisoned. In other words, detention in police custody was the unique unstable equilibrium which the kindred rallied to stabilize. Stability for the better in the form of release, or stability for the worse in the form of sentencing to prison, each caused the rallying instinct to rapidly evaporate.

For now, the four men were in police custody, and the rallying was on in Idumu-uya. The main objective was to raise a substantial sum of money that would be enough to grease their way to and through the divisional police headquarters. For their part, the police were in no hurry to charge the men to court. Irrespective of what the finer points of the law said, they intended to hold the suspects for some time, knowing that sooner or later, their relatives would come forward to seek their release. A few relatives arrived on the morning after the arrests. But they were there mainly to provide the material needs of the suspects, since the police, by default or design, did not provide much in the form of food, drink, clothing or medicaments for detainees. Those who would come to seek their release would come later, appropriately equipped with heavy pockets to match their heavy hearts.

Three days after the arrests, the people of Idumu-uya began to feel their way towards the police headquarters, timid and tentative. They knew from experience that in such matters, a frontal approach might scare the police and cause them to retreat into officialdom, with adverse consequences for the suspects. An indirect approach was much preferred by all sides. A little inquiry pointed Idumu-uya in the direction of Robert Udene, the fixer in police matters. He was the soft underbelly through which the police could be approached in such troubles.

Udene was not a policeman, but he was as good as one. Maybe even better. He knew their ways, he knew their limitations, and he knew the full extent of their lust for money. Just as important, he knew how to get them what they wanted in order to slake their thirst. Udene was aware of the desperate limits to which ordinary people were willing to go to satisfy police greed, so long as they could obtain the freedom of detained relatives. All this made Udene the ideal intermediary between the greedy, but wary, police and the desperate populace. Each haul of detainees meant new business for Udene, and eventually, a plentiful harvest for the policemen.

A small delegation was sent from Idumu-uya to begin work on securing the release of the detainees. Okafor, the leader of the delegation, met with Udene. He was duly informed that it required 30,000 naira to secure the release of each of the three suspected murderers. Iwegbu's brother, who was only being held as a surety, could be released on payment of 15,000 naira. As with most transactions among Enuani people, Okafor tried to haggle to beat down the prices. But Udene cut him off brusquely, warning that these were fixed prices. It was take it or leave it.

In all the hushed discussion, Udene did not say, and Okafor dared not ask, who or what the money was meant for. It was presumed that each side understood. Nor did anybody dare to raise the legal niceties: whether detainees accused of murder were entitled to bail at all; whether police bail, when it could be granted, was not meant to be granted free of charge; whether the individuals would be charged to court before release; and even whether the release would mean a dropping of the charges, or simply represented bail. For now, Okafor wanted to secure release at all costs. And Udene was anxious to clinch a deal for his own reasons. Mutual silence was the best tactic.

After the discussion, Okafor paid a visit to the office of the senior police officer in charge of the case. That, after all, was the legally proper place to discuss the release of his relatives. But the real center of action lay elsewhere, with Udene. Okafor need not have bothered going to this policeman's office. All he got from the officer were strictly official pronouncements and interpretations of the law. A stiff upper lip. There was no mention of Udene, and no mention of any monetary precondition for the release of the detainees. The veil of deniability was well and truly in place, even though everybody could see through it.

Okafor conveyed Udene's message back to the expectant hearts and ears of Idumu-uya. Their collective purse, which was maintained for this sort of emergency, was far from buoyant and could not cope with the level of funds required. Fund raising, including borrowing from external sources, was set in motion.

By the time one market week elapsed, Idumu-uya had raised about two-thirds of the sum stipulated by Udene. With a nod from the kindred elders, Okafor left with this sum and a small delegation, to see if the money could achieve the desired purpose. It could not. Udene and his invisible handlers were driving a hard bargain. It was all or nothing as far as the money was concerned. No discounts.

The delegation returned to Anibaba with the money, but without the detainees or any promise of their release. However, the delegation also returned with something else, quite unpleasant. A further element of menace had been conveyed to Okafor and his delegation: if the release of the detainees was not secured within five days, their case would be transferred to the State headquarters.

This would entail a quantum jump in the terms and conditions needed for their release, if release could be secured at all.

How could they, Idumu-uya, risk having their relatives swallowed up in the bottomless pit of the mysterious Western legal system? They must do everything to rectify the situation, if only to avoid the wrath of their ancestors' spirits. Idumu-uya scurried around in desperation, looking for funds to solve their problem. Long-term savings, stashed away in mattresses and in ceilings, were ferreted out and pressed into service. Yams that were reserved for the approaching famine period or awaiting higher prices, were rushed to market and sold for whatever they could fetch. Long-forgotten debts, owed by others to Idumu-uya folk, were dusted up and aggressively retrieved. Emissaries were sent to Idumu-uya sons and daughters living in the cities to collect whatever donations could be had.

By the fourth day after the abortive last trip, the money was complete. Okafor and his party once again journeyed to the divisional headquarters, confident that they would succeed this time. But they had difficulty making contact with Udene who had traveled out of town and would not be back till evening. The option of approaching the police directly with the money was totally out of the question. That would blow everybody's cover and stiffen police resistance.

At about 5 p.m., Udene returned. Whispered discussions took place in one corner of a pepper-soup restaurant. The money was handed over to Udene for onward transmission. There was some measure of apprehension in handing over the money to Udene. Apart from his word, there was no corroboration as yet from any other source that the payment would secure the desired release of the detainees. There was always the risk of a double-cross. Certainly, the police were not talking, and seemed impenetrable except through Udene. So, the Idumu-uya delegation resigned itself to the risk, content only in the fact that everybody else in the town assured them of Udene's ability to deliver in such matters. His track record spoke for him.

Udene asked the Idumu-uya delegation to wait for him at the restaurant, while he left with the money, presumably for the police officer's house. He returned in a little over an hour. He announced that the money had been transmitted, and the expected release of the detainees would surely take place. But not till the following day. The news was good for Okafor, except for the last part. Indeed, he grew suspicious and uneasy. Having parted with the receipt-less money, he needed more definite confirmation that it was achieving its purpose. Udene sensed the unease, and offered to take Okafor, alone, to visit the senior police officer in charge.

When they got to the police officer's house, Udene went in, while Okafor waited outside. Soon, Udene came out with the officer, whom Okafor recognized. Greetings were exchanged, and the three of them conferred briefly under the umbrella tree. Okafor took a deep breath of relief when the officer confirmed that the detainees would be released the following day. Of course, the officer would not confirm having received any money, and all three of them avoided any mention of it whatsoever. But Okafor felt reassured. The stiff upper lip which he had encountered in this officer on previous occasions was now the source of casual banter and even friendliness. Such is the mellowing magic of money.

As promised, the three murder suspects were released to Okafor around noon the following day. Iwegbu's brother, too, was released, even though Iwegbu himself, in lieu of whom he was arrested, had not come forward to turn himself in. Indeed, Iwegbu emerged from hiding shortly after the terms for the release of the detainees became known. The terms did not include his own surrender, and neither he nor Idumu-uya wanted him to complicate matters by volunteering arrest. It was best to let the matter lie. And so far, it was lying well enough for Iwegbu.

The three murder suspects returned to Anibaba, still basking in the glory of their sordid deed. Any hope that their detention for about two weeks would make them repentant, such hope was totally misplaced. True, they paraded mosquito bites and slight emaciation as physical evidence of the harsh conditions in the police cells. But their diabolical spirits remained unsubdued and unbowed. Any realization that they did wrong was still very far from them. With crass insensitivity towards the financial and physical hardship which they had inflicted on Idumu-uya, they still boasted openly about how they had dispensed justice to Nwafor the unjust; and how nobody, not even the police, could prevent them from dealing ruthlessly with the enemies of Idumu-uya.

***

Nwafor's body was returned to Anibaba four days after it was taken away by the police ambulance. Apparently, its handling in the intervening days was less than satisfactory, and deterioration had commenced. There was, therefore, considerable rush in the burial arrangements, once the body was returned to Anibaba. The burial ceremonies were brief and sparsely attended, inevitably affected by the cloud of controversy surrounding the death.

Nwafor's relatives, licking their wounds, did their best to bear their grief with fortitude. But they were never allowed to live it down, given the apparent freedom and boastfulness of the supposed murderers of their brother. They were too confused and dispirited to contemplate revenge. While some of the hot-blooded younger ones advocated immediate retaliation, the more enlightened ones, including the Obi, wanted to wait and see the eventual fate of the murderers. The wizened old men advocated caution, preaching that time would take care of matters.

As the weeks rolled by, it became clear that the retribution which Nwafor's relatives desired was indeed being exacted on their behalf by a most unforeseen source. The police. And not in a straight forward manner as the law would dictate. But in a curious round-about way. Four weeks after the alleged murderers were released from custody, the police again swooped on Idumu-uya. This time, they took away a total of seven persons: Iwegbu, his first wife, and five others including, quite curiously, a husband and wife who only returned to the village two weeks earlier, after a continuous absence of many years in Lagos. The three alleged murderers were present during the raid but none of them was taken away. Surely, the officer who led the swoop recognized them, exchanged greetings with them, and even remarked to one of them about how much weight he had gained since his release from detention.

The police explained to the people of Idumu-uya that those taken away this time were to assist police in the "on-going" investigation into Nwafor's murder. In short, they were being taken away for questioning. They were not under arrest. But people who knew the ways of the police did not let this assurance deceive them into thinking that securing the release of these individuals would be easy. They knew that the police net, just like the government treasury, was constructed with a one-way valve at its entrance: easy to get in, but very difficult to get out. It was almost irrelevant that among the several persons taken away, only Iwegbu had any connection with the killing of Nwafor.

Suspicions were confirmed when the seven persons were clamped into police cells as soon as they arrived at the divisional headquarters. Nobody even pretended to go through the motions of interrogating them. Quite the opposite. Almost immediately after they arrived, the policemen who brought them vanished into thin air, leaving the hapless villagers virtually incommunicado, but confined all the same.

One day passed, and still nothing happened. Two days. Three. It was becoming painfully clear to Idumu-uya that the seven persons were under arrest, if not *de jure*, at least *de facto*. The usual retinue of relatives who hung around the station to provide human services for the detainees had arrived from home on the very day of the latest arrests. They were doing their usual job. But by the fourth day, they were growing tired and restive. They sent word home to Idumu-uya that their relations were being detained, but that little else was being done with them. They were not charged; they were not questioned; they were not even asked to make written or oral statements. It seemed that their relatives were being detained for nothing.

No. Their relatives were not being detained for nothing. There was definitely some sense in the ongoing madness. On the fifth day, apparently tired of waiting to be contacted, Udene showed up at the police station. He sent word, through one of the distraught relatives, that Okafor should come and see him. The message was duly relayed, and Okafor needed nobody to tell him what the game was all about. Dutifully, he notified the elders of Idumu-uya about the message he received, and of his apprehensions as to what it might portend.

Exactly a week after the latest police swoop, Okafor traveled to meet with Udene. And surely enough, there was a feeling of *déjà vu* about the whole matter. The terrain and procedures were not unlike what they had traversed less than two months earlier. Only the details differed.

"You know that Iwegbu is the most closely connected with the murder incident," declared Udene, as he huddled with Okafor. "It will require the highest amount to secure his release."

"What of the others?" asked Okafor.

"Each of the others will attract a lower, flat rate. That's very lenient, you know."

"And what of the unfortunate couple who had not been to Anibaba for nearly a year prior to the murder? They only arrived some weeks after the incident."

"They too will have to pay the flat rate," Udene replied. "The law is an ass, you know," he added with a wry cheeky chuckle.

Okafor could not have agreed more with this conclusion. It was not only the law that was an ass. Some of its enforcers apparently were asses just as much.

Taxing themselves to the limit, after they thought they had already done so, Idumu-uya began frantic fundraising again. They raised about three-quarters of what was required for each person's release, leaving each nuclear family to make up the shortfall. Since the various families mustered this shortfall at different rates, the detainees were not released all at once. As each person's ransom arrived to Udene, he or she was released. First to go home was Iwegbu with his wife. Apparently he was the only one among the detainees who was psychologically and financially prepared for an encounter with the police after Nwafor's murder. He was able to pay up quickly. The others gained their freedom, days or weeks later. Nobody questioned the reverse justice where the individual with the closest connection to the crime was the first to be freed.

Modern or traditional justice, either way you lose

Over the next nine months, Idumu-uya went through several recurrent cycles of the same unpleasant refrain: police swoop, detention, negotiation with Udene, ransom payment, and freedom for the detainees. The pattern of detention was indiscriminate. Almost anybody could be picked up in any particular swoop. And the likelihood of being detained bore little relationship to one's connection to the killing of Nwafor, even though the investigation of this murder was the reason given for the detentions. Before long, Idumu-uya came to see the police swoops as simply fund-raising exercises, embarked upon by the policemen whenever they were low on cash, or their salaries needed to be augmented. Nobody was ever charged, and nobody ever appeared in court. In all, twenty-six different Idumu-uya villagers, most of them totally innocent, were squeezed through the rigors and indignity of detention followed by extortion. And all that trouble without in any way furthering the cause of justice, which was to apprehend the killers of Nwafor Isieche.

Nor were the three alleged murderers totally spared the inflictions of the corrupt system. After their initial detention and release, they were picked up again and detained along with others, during the third police swoop on Idumu-uya. As before, they had to pay their way out of detention. But after their release this time, their freedom seemed permanent, and the police seemed more interested in making hay from those more distantly connected with the murder.

Nwafor's relatives and friends were content to see Idumu-uya suffer and squirm at the hands of the police. No further retaliation was necessary, since Nwafor's murder was being sufficiently avenged by the police harassment of Iwegbu and Idumu-uya. Nwafor's people knew that at the individual level, the innocent were being punished just as much as the guilty. But in their view, Idumu-uya deserved all it was getting. Karma was catching up with them.

The Obi himself was torn between two loyalties. As a relative of Nwafor, he privately relished the troubles and tribulations of Idumu-uya. They deserved all they were getting. But as the Obi of the entire town, he resented that innocent subjects of his were being punished, and the wrong people were reaping monetary rewards as a result of the crime.

One evening during the turbulent times, Uti paid a visit to the Obi. Uti was seeking the Obi's consent to fix the date for Uti's personal *Ikenga* festival. This was a semi-formal visit, so Uti took along some kolanuts and palm wine. The substance of the visit went well and was brief. So, the pair had extra time to chat about other matters.

The Obi asked Uti about the latest developments regarding Nwafor's death. After all, Uti was present at the very birth of this crisis. And as Nwafor's faithful friend, he surely must be following all the twists and turns of these events.

"I really feel sorry the way things are going in Anibaba," Uti lamented.

"It's giving me sleepless nights," the Obi replied. "It seems that each day brings on new problems and new strife in my domain."

"And poor Nwafor. I can't imagine that such a peaceful man died such a tragic death."

"Yet, his death has not brought peace to Anibaba."

"And look at those three young men that killed him. They've been roaming the streets for years."

"I'm sorry that there're so many such jobless young men in Anibaba," the Obi said. "Their only job is drinking, in addition to smoking all sorts of things."

"It's the drinking and smoking that emboldens them in their atrocities. They are jobless and useless. They refuse to engage in farm work like us and our ancestors. They claim that farm work is too tedious, and below their dignity."

"Yet, what's their alternative?" the Obi asked.

"The alternative is to get salaried employment in the modern set-up. But to do that, you need schooling and education. These roaming ruffians have neither."

"They've abandoned our traditional occupation of farming, but cannot qualify for the modern-day occupations. What a pity. All they can do is roam around and cause trouble."

"Like in Nwafor's case," Uti concluded.

"Any time these hooligans find people quarreling, they go in and worsen it."

"That's surely what they do."

The Obi shook his head, took a sip of his palm wine, and stared blankly at the floor for a few moments.

"But this enmity between Idumu-uya and Nwafor's kindred, when do you think it will end?" the Obi asked, looking up at Uti.

"Your guess is as good as mine," Uti replied.

"And now with Nwafor being murdered, new bitterness has been added to the situation."

"It's worse than before. I don't expect a settlement in my lifetime."

"Nor in mine."

"But don't you think that it's the police that are fanning the flames of the fire that is burning us," Uti suggested.

"Yes. They're the breeding ground for corruption."

"But it's not the police alone," Uti continued. "Look at us here in Anibaba. Even our Onotu is corrupt. The old traditional system used to dispense good justice. But now it's corrupt. And the Western police system that replaced it is corrupt also. We lose both ways. Where can a person find justice in this world?"

"This thing we call corruption is like cancer. It infects everything, and is hard to cure. It even has stages of its own, just like cancer."

"Tell me more," Uti urged.

"Let me tell you a story about the various stages of damage that corruption can inflict," the Obi said, settling further into his heavily padded chair. "It's a long story. Are you sure you have enough time?"

"I've got plenty of time. Please go ahead."

"At a certain time in the next district, the rate of road accidents was alarming, primarily because most of the vehicles were in disrepair. The police set up check-points on the roads to check on the condition of passing vehicles. Whenever a driver came along the road, his vehicle would be inspected. If the vehicle was fault-free, the driver was allowed to go without any molestation. But if the vehicle was defective, the driver was given a ticket and paid a fine to the state. Only the guilty were punished, not the innocent."

"Great."

"But then, corruption crept into the police force. They changed their style. Now, fault-free vehicles were still allowed to go free. But for faulty vehicles, there was a new twist. The drivers were obliged to pay a bribe to the police, and then be allowed to go on. This is the first stage or first degree of corruption damage. It punishes the guilty and lets the innocent go free, just like the normal legal system. But significantly, it diverts the money into private pockets."

"So, the state suffers," Uti cut in. "The revenue goes into the pockets of the corrupt officials instead of going to the state."

"I'm glad you're following the tale," the Obi added, as Uti leaned forward for more. "After some weeks, the rate of road accidents began to drop. Most of the drivers had taken correction, and nearly every vehicle that came through was faultless. But the corrupt officers noticed that their daily takings were diminishing because very few vehicles had faults. So, in order to maintain their revenue and satisfy their corrupt appetite, the officers started to harass the drivers of faultless vehicles."

"Some kind of entrapment."

"Yes. Innocent drivers were made to pay bribes for imagined or minor faults. This is the second degree of corruption damage. In this case, the innocent suffer along with the guilty. In addition, the state suffers by having the revenue from fines diverted into private pockets."

Uti was now starting to wonder what all this had to do with Anibaba, or Idumu-uya. But the Obi continued with his tale.

"Since every vehicle that came through had to pay, whether there was a fault or not, what did the drivers do? Of course, they no longer bothered to maintain their vehicles in faultless condition, since a bribe was demanded irrespective of the condition of the vehicle. So, most of the vehicles were allowed to fall into disrepair again. And with most vehicles in disrepair, the accident rate went up again. Back to the original bad situation. The primary purpose of setting up the checkpoints was thoroughly defeated. This is the third degree of corruption damage. It is where the entire system has become infected by the cancer, and comes tumbling down. The state suffers, the innocent suffer, the guilty suffer, and the entire system is threatened."

"You're talking like a professor now," Uti said, thoroughly impressed by the Obi's logic.

The Obi paused, long enough to catch his breath.

"Now, you wonder what all this has to do with Anibaba," the Obi continued. "You've seen the activities of the corrupt police officers in connection with Nwafor's death. You've also seen the detentions of Idumu-uya folk. These are all clear manifestations of the third degree of corruption damage. Right here in our town. Fine and bail revenues due to the state are being denied it. The innocent are being punished just as much as the guilty, or even more. There's no incentive for good behavior. So, impunity reigns. Murderers are being allowed to roam free, and the entire system of justice has collapsed. It's been rubbished by the greedy onslaught of these officers."

"Unfortunately, our own traditional justice system has also been rubbished," said Uti. "Look at Onotu. I long for the olden days when Onotu was Onotu. Onotu then was fearless and incorruptible."

"Our development is going in reverse gear," the Obi lamented. "In fact, I heard somebody call it de-development. When the people lost faith in Onotu as a source of justice, we all pinned our hope on the modern system that the white man brought. But look what has happened. The people have also lost faith in the ability of the police and courts to deliver justice. There's nothing left. Our ancestors must be laughing at us now. I fear that more people will now take the law into their own hands, with impunity."

The somber inference with which the Obi concluded his treatise struck a particular chord with Uti. He recalled afresh how and why

Nwafor, his friend, lost confidence in the traditional system of justice, as symbolized by Onotu; how, as a result, Nwafor took the law into his own hands and burned Iwegbu's barn; how, in retribution, Nwafor was murdered by Iwegbu's kin; and how finally, the police got into the act and served their own purposes instead of the purposes of justice.

As he adjusted his loin cloth, preparatory to bidding the Obi good-bye, Uti asked emptily:

"If the people have lost faith in the traditional system of justice, and they have lost faith in the police and the modern system of justice, where then does that leave us?"

"We're neither here nor there," the Obi concluded ruefully. "We're stranded in a no-man's-land. You remember what our people say about the bat. Bats are not birds of the air since they have teeth; and they are not ground animals since they fly. Some even say that this ambiguous situation is the reason why bats don't perch upright. Instead, bats hang upside down. We're just like bats. We're neither birds of the air, nor animals on the ground. *Ụsụ abụna anụ enu ma ọ bụna anụ anị.*"

"But why must we also hang upside down like the bat?"

The question dangled hauntingly in the air. Nobody attempted to answer it.

☼ Chapter 4

Ada's Day: Toils And Travails Of Enuani Village Womanhood

If you accused Ada of being lazy, you immediately became a liar. Scratching out a living as a poor village wife and mother permitted no room for laziness. Accuse her of worrying too much about the family's daily domestic needs, and you were closer to the truth. Her husband, Ebo, was equally hardworking, equally fretful, and equally resigned to their fate as poor Enuani village folk.

On this day, Ada woke up at the first crowing of the rooster in the early morning. In the pre-dawn darkness, she immediately embarked on sweeping and cleaning around the house. As usual, she started with the kitchen area and the living room, careful not to wake those still sleeping in the bedrooms. Ada hated a dirty house, and was very meticulous in her daily cleaning of both the house and the compound. By the time Ebo woke up, she was scrubbing the mud floors of the veranda with the red clay suspension (*ité uno*). This was the last cleaning activity before she moved on to other chores of her busy day.

While Ada toiled around the house, Ebo prepared for a long day of hard work at the farm. He charged his gourd full of drinking water and obtained a glowing ember from the overnight fire. His multi-purpose farm bag contained all sorts of things, including his tiny snuff bottle, and a piece of kolanut. Slinging the bag over his shoulder, he was quickly on his way. Dawn had not yet broken on the village as he passed through it, but a couple of early risers were also stirring in their houses. The two-mile distance to the farm was covered at a brisk walking pace, all the time swinging the glowing ember vigorously to prevent the fire from dying out.

Ebo encountered only two sets of humans on the way to the farm. The first was Okeleke, trudging home gleefully under the weight of some unfortunate casualties of a successful night of hunting.

"*Nnua!*" Ebo grunted the usual greeting of welcome for the homeward-bound hunter.

"*Ndo-o,*" was the equally grunted reply acknowledging the greeting.

Ebo would have loved to know what animal Okeleke was carrying in his bag, but he managed to restrain himself from asking. The solemnity of the pre-dawn period made it improper to engage in more detailed interaction.

The other humans that Ebo encountered were a group of two women and a child who had braved the early-morning cold for a dash to fetch water from the stream. Ebo recognized the women. But again, the greetings were sparse, almost perfunctory. Each of the women was having enough trouble coping with the large water calabashes balanced precariously on their heads as they headed home at a brisk pace. They too were in no mood for conversation or extended greetings.

Once at the farm, the first order of business was to make a fire, using the glowing ember. The glow left in the ember was just barely enough to start the fire which would be Ebo's lifeline to preparing his lunch later. Given its importance, village farmers seldom entrusted the ember to children that accompanied them to the farm. In an era when safety matches were unknown or scarce, the glowing ember featured significantly in the prospects for lunch on the farm.

As soon as the fire got going, Ebo carefully sharpened his two machetes on a nearby stone whose surface clearly indicated that it had habitually been used for the purpose. And then to work. Today's tasks included weeding on the yam plot, planting some cassava and, if time permitted, procuring a few more stakes from the bush for staking the yams.

Ebo worked diligently all morning. He knew by habit that a farmer's best productivity came in the cooler morning hours, before the day's heat set in. He worked tirelessly, stopping only occasionally for a sip of water from the gourd or a pinch of snuff for his nose. Occasionally, too, he sought solace in a nibble, one small piece at a time, from a piece of kolanut which was strategically tucked away in his scanty work attire. But by mid-morning, thoughts were turning to more substantial sustenance. Man could not live by kolanut alone. A plump tuber of yam was produced from his bag, and found its way onto the fire. Work continued while the yam roasted.

At about 11 a.m., it was time for Ebo to take his version of a brunch break. The roasted yam was plucked from the fire, the charred exterior was scraped off, and the yam was sliced into manageable pieces. Given Ebo's state of exhaustion and hunger, there was no waiting for the yam to cool down. It was devoured with huffing and puffing at the highest tolerable temperature. Although Ebo sometimes brought palm oil for the yam brunch at the farm, on this day there was none. No oil. No salt. No pepper. Just plain roasted yam. Shorn of all relish, the yam was not particularly appetizing to Ebo. But he was content to manage along, secure in the knowledge that a full-blown delicious supper awaited him at home at the end of the day. Ada, his faithful wife, would see to that, as she had done for some twenty years. So, for now, the roasted yam would serve its purpose of staving off hunger and boosting Ebo's energy reserves for a few more hours of tedious farm work.

Shortly after refueling, Ebo stretched out horizontally under the oilbean (*ụgba*à) tree, for a bit of rest. It was the height of the rainy season. So, the tree was in full leaf and provided adequate shade. Looking up at it from his lying position, Ebo could see the flat brown fruits on the tree. In a few months, these fruits would be fully formed, ready to disperse their seeds explosively during the dry season. For many years, Ebo and his family relished the *ụgba*à condiment prepared from the fermented seeds of this particular tree.

Oilbean pods (Ụgbaà)

Ebo's rest, scrappy as it was, did not last long. Barely ten minutes after he lay down, there was a noise at the outer edge of the farm. Ebo woke up, but remained completely still as he tried to discern the source and nature of the noise. A few seconds later, the family dog appeared, wagging its tail appreciatively and then sniffing around for scraps of the roasted yam. Jebby often came to the farm alone, trailing the scent of members of the family. So, there was no surprise or alarm in Jebby's sudden appearance. As Ebo rose from his horizontal position to welcome Jebby, he was startled by a distinct human call from one corner of the farm.

"Ho! Hooo!" the person yelled.

The voice was unmistakable. It was Ada.

"Nne-Uli, *Nnụa!*" He welcomed her.

"I thought I should surprise you," she said.

"You certainly succeeded."

"I not only succeeded; I caught you napping. Is that what you do on the farm all day? You wake up late at home, then you come to the farm to sleep some more."

Of course, she was only teasing, since she knew that Ebo usually did a lot of work before he permitted himself any meaningful rest. He understood that she was joking. A loud explosion of laughter was the only answer he gave to her question.

"You must have changed your mind," he said.

"About what?"

"Didn't you tell me that you wanted to wash some clothes this morning, and then extract oil from the oil palm bunches I harvested last week?"

"Yes. And that's exactly what I did. It's all done," she said.

"All done? So fast?"

"Yes. You know Uli is on holidays from her boarding school. Her help made the work go very quickly. Aren't we blessed with a dutiful daughter?"

"God bless her."

Ada sat down next to Ebo, who then offered her a leftover piece of the roasted yam. But she declined.

"So, what are you going to do at the farm today," Ebo asked. "Will you help me weed the yam plot?"

"No! No! No!" she protested. "You know that maintaining the yam plot is a man's job. At least in Enuani."

"Then, you're just going to watch me while I work?"

"Yes! Watching you should be fun," she teased. "But in between watching you, I'll attend to some womanly chores around the farm."

"Like what, today?"

"I'll finish extracting the *egusi* melon seeds. Then I'll harvest some okra for our supper tonight."

"Okra?"

"Yes, okra. Pounded yam with okra soup is what we'll have for supper. I know it's your favorite meal."

Ebo smiled, in gleeful anticipation of his favorite dish for supper. That would be a huge contrast to the sparse roasted yam that was sustaining him on the farm.

Suddenly, Ada got up.

"Sitting near you here is making both of us lazy," she said.

"Maybe you. But not me."

"Well, I must hurry. I've got so many other things to do after I finish here at the farm."

"And you still plan to go to the Eke market today?"

"You don't need to ask. Do I ever miss the Eke market?"

"I just thought I should ask."

"Whenever it's Eke day, going to market is a must for me. It's the last big task of the day before I come home to cook supper."

Ebo got up from his sitting position. They hugged each other, and then proceeded in opposite directions where their respective farm chores lay. They worked at separate tasks in separate parts of the farm, but never really lost contact with each other. They telegraphed communication back and forth. An occasional word of encouragement, a song, or even a shared joke ensured that the two souls labored as one under the unrelenting tropical sun.

 In a little over an hour, Ada finished her assignment and was ready to go home. She invited Ebo to come over to her location, so they could bid each other a proper goodbye. Ebo got there and saw her standing

beside a loosely tied bunch of firewood which she intended to take home.

"Are you sure you can carry all this on your head?" Ebo asked.

"I'll try to manage. There's no firewood left in the house."

"Be careful. Anyway, let me help you tie it properly so it's easier for you to carry."

Ebo re-tied the firewood bunch. He hugged Ada, and then helped her position the bunch on her head for the journey home. The extracted *egusi* melon and the okra were carried in a bag which Ada hung on her shoulder. Jebby led the way as Ada picked her cautious path home, leaving Ebo to put finishing touches to his day's labor.

Ada was dead tired when she got home. The labors of the morning and at the farm were taking their toll. Moreover, she had eaten only scantily all day. For breakfast, she and Uli shared the remnants of the previous day's pounded yam (*nni-ọla*); for lunch, it was a few spoonfuls of *gari* (toasted cassava flour) in water. Like Ebo, she pinned her hopes for culinary satisfaction on the all-satisfying supper, yet to come. Delicious okra soup and pounded yam were beckoning.

By midafternoon, the Eke market was beginning to take shape. Ada's friend from the neighboring compound hailed her from the street as the neighbor made her way to the market. Ada's all-day plan was that she would go to the market as well. But now, she was tired. Dead tired.

"Uli!" she called out to her daughter. "Come and sit here beside me." Uli came running, and did as she was told.

"My daughter, think of all the chores you and I have done today."

Uli nodded her head, not quite sure where her mother was going with this conversation.

"Yes," continued the mother. "We've done so much today. Too much, perhaps. I'm now very tired."

Uli nodded her head again, still not saying a word.

"I think I'll skip the Eke market today," said the mother abruptly.

"Yes, I think you need some rest," Uli finally said.

"I think so too. But tell me, when does your holiday finish for you to return to school?"

"In three days' time."

"Three days? That's before the next Eke market day."

"Yes, Mama."

"I didn't think it was so soon."

"Yes. Time flies."

"So, this is the last Eke before you return to school."

"I think so."

"This is our last chance to sell the yams that your father put aside for your school fees."

There was a pause, while each one contemplated the situation.

"I can take them to Eke market today and sell them myself," Uli ventured.

But Ada was cool to the offer. She knew from painful experience that Uli did not have the haggling skills required to sell the yams at a decent price. The truth was dawning on Ada. The thought that this was the last market day before Uli's departure made it clear to her that her options were limited. Like it or not, tired or not, Ada had to go to the market that day, if only to sell the yams to meet Uli's schooling needs.

Neither Ebo nor Ada earned a salary. Money matters usually had to be solved by selling some of their farm produce. For this occasion, it was the yam tubers which Ebo commissioned Ada to sell at the market.

After casting around listlessly for a short while, Ada got down to the serious business of preparing for the market. The all-important yams were loaded into a basket which Uli would help deliver to the marketplace. Into Ada's large market calabash basin (*ugba afịa*), she loaded other minor items: a packet of *egusi* melon seeds, two bunches of bitterleaf, three bottles of palm oil from the morning's extraction, a bottle of drinking water, and some okra left over from what was sequestered for supper.

"Mama, do you think it will be a good market day?" Uli asked, as she folded the cloth pad for carrying the basket of yams on her head.

"I hope so," replied Ada. "But I worry."

"About what, Mama."

"I worry that I have to sell all the yams. All of them."

"You will," assured Uli.

"I must. That's the only way to be sure of your school fees."

"You'll sell them all, Mama."

"I think I will. But it may require my staying at the market till late."

"Don't worry. I'll stay there with you, as long as it takes," offered Uli.

"Thank you, my child. But if it gets too late, your father will already be home, hungry and waiting for supper. You know he eats very little at the farm. And I've already told him to expect delicious okra soup tonight."

"Yes, he likes that. But he gets angry if he has to wait too long. What shall we do?"

"The yams must be sold," said Ada. "So, I think we'll do what we did last time."

Uli got the idea and remembered the last time she and Ada used that idea. They were caught between two unpalatable options: return home early to prepare supper but risk not selling all the yams; or stay on to sell all the yams and risk angering a hungry Ebo by delaying supper. What they did last time was for Uli alone to return early from the market. She would commence the preparation of supper, well before Ada returned. Uli would prepare the pounded yam, but leave the delicate task of preparing the soup for Ada to undertake whenever she returned from the market. It sounded like a good strategy.

Eke market was in full swing when Uli and Ada arrived there. Nearly all the traders with designated stalls had occupied their places. Somewhere in the center was the special stall for the Ọmụ, the village queen who presided over the markets and women's affairs. Overflow traders and people from other towns pitched their wares at the outskirts of the market. Some aggressive sellers had little hand bells with which they advertised their wares. This village market did not have sections for various commodities. Each trader simply displayed what they had wherever they could find space, or even hawked them around from place to place. Customers drifted up and down through the narrow alleys, picking their way carefully so as not to upset the delicately displayed merchandise. Also drifting up and down was the occasional aggressive goat, insistent on taking a bite from displayed items, and content to endure the flailing whips of the angry merchants. Eke market constituted controlled chaos.

Ada and Uli picked their way to their usual stall and unburdened themselves of their wares. They displayed their merchandise in the best positions to appeal to customers. Uli then took on the role of a megaphone, breathlessly shouting enticements to passersby to come and buy the best yams on earth. Like an unctuous auctioneer, she gave the impression that your life wouldn't be complete without these very yams.

She soon caught the attention of customers. The first customer came by, looked at the yams, but bought some okra instead. The next customer did not even show any interest in the yams. She went straight to the okra, sized up all that was remaining, and bought them all. Commerce for okra was brisk, but that for yam was so far looking sluggish.

Some relief came when the next couple of customers showed interest in the yams. They engaged Ada in the usual haggling and bargaining until they arrived at a mutually acceptable price. But they wanted the yams on credit. Ada refused. Knowing the pressing cash purpose for which the yams were being sold, how could she sell them on credit? She was also aware that persuading village debtors to pay up was like pulling teeth. So, while the *egusi*, okra, and other smaller items among their wares sold quickly, the yams continued to stare blankly at Ada and Uli. The all-important yams.

About an hour after they arrived, Uli was dispatched to return home. She was mandated to prepare the pounded yam, and was given detailed instructions on which condiments to assemble in anticipation of Ada's preparation of the soup.

Shortly after Uli got home, Ebo dragged himself home from the farm. A tropical squall, brief but heavy, caught him on the way home and drenched him thoroughly. He looked every bit like a scarecrow as he trudged into the family compound. Uli greeted him, but his response was just barely audible. He was not in a talking mood, almost as if his tiredness robbed him of his speech. A quick bath, a bit of rest in his *ọgwa* (outdoor resting house), and off he went to visit a sick relative. Visiting around the village was his usual way of passing the hours before dusk while waiting for supper.

When she returned from the market, Uli busied herself ironing some of her school clothes, and generally getting ready for her impending return to school. But she kept a keen eye on the cranky clock in the living room, a skill she learned from school. At precisely 5:15 p.m., it was time to start cooking.

Some yams were duly peeled, boiled, pounded, and molded into portions. Uli had gone through this process so many times before that she could almost do it with her eyes closed. Then she proceeded to assemble the soup condiments around the fireplace: chopped okra, a slab of locust bean, a long-preserved dry half of rabbit, ground pepper, a much-shriveled slice of onion, some crayfish, a piece of *akanwụ* (potash) to enhance the draw of the okra, palm oil in its usual glass bottle, and salt in its usual plastic container. All the players in the soup symphony were ready and waiting. The conductor, Ada, was yet to return home.

Ebo returned from his excursion just before Uli finished pounding the yam. He now had little to do, than loiter around waiting for the meal to be ready. His visits around the village, perhaps punctuated with a glass of palm wine here and there, seemed to have given him his vigor back. It had at least loosened his tongue, and he chatted with Uli about her impending return to school. But the chat was not spirited. It was only a holding action.

Six o'clock, and still Ada had not returned from the market. Six thirty. A quarter to seven. She normally did not stay this late at the market. But then again, it was not every market day that she had yams that must be disposed of. So, the lateness was understandable. But that was little consolation for Ebo's hungry anticipation.

Finally, out of pity for Ebo, Uli decided to venture into the soup preparation process by herself. She had done it a few times before, with mixed results. So, why not now? As opposed to the traditional process of soup-making, Uli had a style of her own. She basically placed the pot on the fire, added some water, and threw in the condiments all at once. And this included the salt. She had scant regard for the traditional process whereby the condiments went in at different times, and where the salt came at the very end when the soup was done and ready for consumption. So, Uli got the soup going her own way.

The things in the pot had not quite come to a boil when Ada arrived. She was all apologies.

"Nna-Uli, please pardon me," she said breathlessly to Ebo.

"*Nnua*. Welcome back," Ebo replied.

"You see, I had to dispose of those yams at all costs."

"I understand."

"The last yam sold in good time. But Nne-Chime was the buyer and she didn't have enough cash on hand."

"Oh! Nne-Chime! Nobody trusts her. She's full of tricks," said Ebo.

"I didn't trust her either," Ada continued. "I know she's a magnet for debts which she never repays. She claimed that she had enough money at home. So I thought it wise to follow her home to collect the money for the yams. That's why I'm so late in returning home."

"So, did she pay?" asked Ebo.

"Cash on hand," Ada replied. "That's the only way to deal with Nne-Chime. She paid in full."

"I'm happy. Don't worry about your lateness, my dear."

Ebo fully understood Ada's mission at the market. He welcomed her home more in hunger than in anger. Meanwhile, Ada scurried around like a decapitated fowl, trying to make up for lost time. She flung her market wares into a corner, and without even bothering to change her clothes, she dashed to the fireplace to tend the soup. Intermittently, she uttered some form of additional apology aimed in Ebo's direction.

Okra

With the soup maestro now in charge, Uli withdrew into the background, trying to corral some errant chicken that had chosen the wrong place to spend the night. Before long, Ada sensed that the soup was done. And by force of habit, it was time for the salt to go in. So, in went the salt. Uli was not near-by to caution that she had already added salt at the commencement of the soup-making process.

Ada stirred the soup, and as usual, instilled a few drops on her left palm for tasting. She tasted it. Oh no. The soup was thoroughly briny. Even more briny than sea water. Double fault by the cooks led to double salting. There had been an error. Belatedly, Ada called out to Uli to ask if she salted the soup earlier. The affirmative answer explained the serious problem which was now threatening the production of the much-anticipated, long-awaited supper.

It was unimaginable that this, of all days, was the one for a problematic soup to creep into the household's equation. This day that Ebo labored since morning and ate very little. This day that Ada, too, worked so hard, discharging a myriad of unrelated tasks. This day that the supper preparation was running late, and Ebo was at the limits of his hungry endurance. This day of all days. The devil himself could not have cooked up a more bewildering situation.

Panic set in. What to do now? Ada was at her wits' end as to which way to turn. There certainly was not enough time to start a fresh brew of soup. And, in any case, there were no extra soup ingredients and condiments in the house. So, the only viable solution was to try to amend the briny soup.

Water was added to reduce the saltiness. It was still briny; so a little more water was added. The level of brininess was now barely acceptable; but then, the soup became very watery and totally lost its draw. A little more simmering restored a semblance of dignity to the soup. But then, the brininess returned.

Somewhere in the heat of the frenzy, Uli volunteered some advice on how to reduce saltiness in soup. A classmate at school had told her that throwing a large piece of charcoal into the soup would do the trick. Uli had never seen it done before, but she believed it could work. Ada was skeptical. As she rejected the advice, she made it clear that she was in no mood for further experimentation. So, Ada was caught in the middle: between a briny soup and a watery soup. In the end, despite all her culinary gymnastics, the final product had both unwanted characteristics, still watery and still noticeably briny.

After about fifteen minutes of juggling the soup alchemy, Ada finally brought the wretched brew down from the fire. Ebo's soup was dished out in the usual *ọkwa* (large wooden bowl). His meal was assembled in the veranda, on the small table with wobbly legs. Then Uli went inside the house to inform him that his long-expected supper was ready.

Ebo had spent the past few minutes in the inner room, over-indulging in his snuff as a way of managing his hunger. A few violent sneezes cleared his sinuses, but still left his stomach empty. Indeed, each sneeze felt as if it was emptying out whatever was left in his shrunken stomach. He wasted no time in answering the call to the supper table. Here at last, was relief for his hunger. With the appetite of a hungry lion, he came out and took his place at the table, ready to start eating. As usual, Ada had the option of joining him there, or eating separately with Uli, or both. So, Ebo knew he did not have to wait for Ada before he could start eating.

Ada was still busy in the courtyard kitchen area, sorting things out. But she devoted a disproportionate amount of her attention to observing Ebo from a distance. She was apprehensive, but said nothing. She was like a tailor watching a customer's reaction as he tried on a suit on which the tailor had made a dreadful mistake. Or like a barber, who made an awful mistake on the back side of your head, watching you finally take a look in the reverse mirror. In each case, great effort and goodwill were the inputs, but the outcome was bad. There was apprehension arising from uncertainty. Would the supposed beneficiary focus on the greatness of the effort or on the badness of the result? Which way would Ebo choose?

Ada watched Ebo wash his hands. He grabbed his first handful of pounded yam and kneaded it briefly in his right hand. He dipped it in the soup and popped it in his mouth. His immediate reflex was to spit it out, but he restrained himself. He forced himself to swallow it. Then, there was icy silence. His appetite was stopped dead in its tracks. He put the portion of pounded yam that was left in his hand back into the bowl. The soup was as watery as it was briny. It had no redeeming feature. The food was simply not edible.

This was not the meal that Ebo looked forward to as a logical reward for his day's labors. Disappointment mingled with frustration in equal measure. Yet, Ebo knew that this was not the quality of Ada's usual production. So, the disappointment was tinged with a good dose of pity for Ada who had a busy day, and who must be feeling terrible shame for serving up such a lousy meal. There was also self-pity on the part of Ebo. After all, a satisfying meal at the end of the day's labors was not too much to expect.

At this stage, Ebo was still unaware of the circumstances that led to the degradation of the soup. But he was surprised that Ada said nothing. Ada on her part simply watched pensively. Her silence said it all. She, too, was battling with an array of emotions. Sorrow, that the meal she presented failed to impress. Shame, that her womanhood was being compromised by her presenting a sub-standard meal. Pity, that Ebo could not immediately satisfy his desperate hunger. Anxiety, at what Ebo's reaction might be. Anger, that her long day of complicated exertions should have all come to this. But she remained silent.

In two decades of marriage, Ebo and Ada had learned to utilize silence as a form of communication. They could speak to each other through silence. And this was one of those times.

At long last, Ada piped up. Apologetically. Like a cowed dog malingering in the background with its tail between its legs, she began a diffident explanation of the events that culminated in the damaged soup. She had only gone half way with her explanations when Ebo asked her to stop.

"I understand," he broke in. "You don't have to explain anymore."

"Thank you, my dear," she replied meekly.

"Yes, I saw how your day went. How you undertook dozens of tasks one after another. All in an effort to support the family. All with a smile."

"Thank you," she repeated.

"If anything, you should be pitied." He paused briefly, and then continued, "And do you know what?"

"What?"

"I've forgiven you even before you spoke."

"Thank you. I knew you would understand. Thank you."

Forgiveness is one thing, but hunger is quite another thing altogether. Ebo's hunger was still raging and tormenting him. It did not abate. And the meal before him could not satisfy it. Nor could the apologies. Something had to be done.

So, he stepped into the yam store, brought out a large tuber of yam, and gave it to Ada with a familiar wink. The yam was for roasting. The dying embers left over from the soup emergency were put together, supplemented with additional firewood. Soon, a vibrant fire was going again in the courtyard kitchen. The yam was thrown in. With the resurgent kitchen fire casting a heartening glow on the beleaguered faces, the depressed spirits of this hard-pressed family started to lift. Gloom was gradually yielding to hope. Things were definitely looking up again.

As a calming palliative for his hunger, Ada kept Ebo distracted with stories and banter, while the yam roasted. However, she was very careful to stay close to the roasting process, lest something should, again, go wrong. This was her chance to recoup some of the emotional losses of the evening. She went to her pantry and selected the freshest palm oil available, precisely the one she extracted earlier that day.

Roasted yam was the same commodity that Ebo ate for his brunch while working on the farm. He ate it mainly as energy support to carry him through the day's labors. Enjoyment was not his prime objective, and he cared little how it tasted. He ate it simply: without salt, without oil, without pepper. This evening's roasted yam had a different purpose and a different culinary status. It was meant to be enjoyed, to be relished. Ada knew that, and saw to it. The freshest palm oil, fresh pungent pepper, salt (that devilish, whimsical commodity), some fermented *ugbaà*, and even a liberal chunk of dried fish, were all pressed into service to adorn the roasted yam. Ada prepared it just the way she knew Ebo preferred it. Soon, the substitute supper was ready.

This was a time for making up, and Ada was keen to play her part. Partly for this reason, and partly to satiate her own hunger, she did not let Ebo eat alone. She snuggled up beside him at the table, and joined in the modest feast.

Uli watched them from the shadows, keen to learn the lessons that the situation offered. She could not but admire the old-time love that enabled the two parents to surmount a very difficult situation. She also wondered about the excessive tedium of their busy lives. Lives that on the surface appeared rosy, but which were extremely hectic and demanding. Lives that only had simple pleasures like roasted yam to liven them up. Was this the kind of life that she too was growing up to live? At school, she was already getting a glimpse of what looked like a different, less tedious lifestyle. This was a lifestyle that offered a degree of emancipation from the kind of hectic village life that Ada was obliged to live. But the new lifestyle was not without its own baggage of peculiar challenges and difficulties. So, Uli had a choice between the old and the new. Only time would tell how she would choose, and where her choice would lead her.

☼ **SECTION II** ☼

Enuani Traits
[Èmùmé Anyi]

☼ **Chapter 5**

Enuani People And Ethos

There has been considerable debate about the origins of Enuani people, resulting in a continuing struggle with issues of identity and political space. The past origins, present position, and future prospects of Enuani are all subjects of animated discussion. What seems clear is that the various towns and villages in Enuani originated from various places, but have since melded into an identifiable entity. While the debate rages about Enuani origins, it is pertinent to observe certain characteristics that have historically marked the Enuani ethos. These characteristics can best be summarized with the acronym SUPA: Satisfied, Unambitious, Poor, and Arrogant. These epithets are only meant to be descriptive, and are in no way intended to demean or derogate the Enuani people individually or collectively. Even though the characteristics do not apply to every Enuani person, they seem to hold true generally.

"*Satisfied*" means that the Enuani person generally has an outlook of contentment in life. This means that he is prone to being happy even in the face of difficult life circumstances. Part of this derives from a strong belief in *chi*, or personal destiny. There's a pervasive sense of resignation to whatever good or bad that *chi* allows into somebody's life. What cannot be avoided must be taken on with a sense of satisfaction.

Perhaps resulting from being easily contented, the Enuani person is generally *unambitious,* bordering on indolence. Where his kin from east of the Niger River is hustling and scraping to get ahead, the Enuani person is more likely to stand back and contentedly wonder what the fuss is all about. There are exceptions, but the unindustrious, easy-going, attitude of the Enuani person contrasts with the trade-mark industriousness and craftiness of the eastern Igbo. Lacking the hustle of the easterners, and the political privilege of some other groups, it is not surprising that Enuani is caught in the middle, and the Enuani area remains developmentally-challenged.

Given the lack of hustle, it is logical that historically, the typical Enuani person has been *poor.* Despite the huge amount of natural resources with which they are endowed, the Enuani people have historically lived in penury. Worse still, the political cohesiveness that is needed to lift them out of poverty has been constantly frustrated by a sense of contentment and a false feeling of security. This has enabled the poverty to persist and propagate from generation to generation.

If you expect a people that are poor and unindustrious to be humble, the Enuani people surprise you with the opposite. Both individually and collectively, Enuani people are a very

 proud people. Some might say *arrogant*. Others have called them haughty, conceited, and unbowed. Poor-and-proud is one way to describe the Enuani people. Many jobs that other people accept and do, the Enuani youth would treat with disdain, considering such jobs to be *infra dig*, beneath their dignity. The groveling gofer life is certainly not for them. As a result, many of the artisan jobs in the Enuani area are performed, not by Enuani persons, but by artisans from other ethnic groups, mostly the eastern Igbo. Meanwhile, hordes of Enuani youth are going about looking pretty, and sneering superciliously at those doing the artisan jobs. This ethos of no-hustle arrogance is shared by the Onitsha, Ogbaru, and Oguta people, three Enuani-related groups that happen to live east of the Niger.

Industrious or not, Enuani people historically spared no effort in the area of cleanliness. They were very meticulous in keeping their persons and surroundings clean. Dawn each day ushered in extensive cleaning of the house and the surrounding compound. In the traditional mud houses, sweeping was followed by scrubbing of the floors and walls with the red clay suspension, a procedure called *ite ụnọ*. Household refuse was collected and dumped in a designated spot, *ikpo ntụ*. At the personal level, each day started with a thorough cleaning of the teeth using a chewing stick (*atụ*). Bathing occurred at least once a day, usually at the end of the day's farm work. This rule was observed even during water scarcity at the height of the dry season. The cleanliness trait in Enuani people is perhaps consistent with their proud demeanor.

It's important to point out one trait which Enuani people have manifested since the second half of the 20th century. It is the ease with which they are willing to cast away key elements of their culture. We can illustrate this with *ákwà ọcha*, the native white cloth which is worn toga-like by Enuani men and as a waist wrapper by the women. For centuries, this cloth has been the identifying garb of most Enuani people. It has been their sartorial totem through the ages, woven by Enuani people and worn by them with pomp and pride. No other attire occupies this position. Yet, one is alarmed by the extent to which Enuani people have abandoned *ákwà ọcha* in the last half century and replaced it with clothing borrowed from other lands.

The first stage in the abandonment of *ákwà ọcha* occurred in the second half of the 20th century when fewer and fewer Enuani people undertook the weaving of the cloth. The art of weaving *ákwà ọcha*, previously so prominent in places like Ubulu-Ukwu, progressively became a lost art among Enuani people. The vacuum created was filled by the non-Enuani Egbira people from around Okene in Kogi State, a long distance away from the heart of Enuani. The Egbira produced delicately decorated *ákwà ọcha* specifically targeted for the Enuani markets. By the end of the 20th century, virtually all the *ákwà ọcha* sold in local Enuani markets were produced in Egbiraland. Enuani people did not take notice of this anomalous shift in the base of production, or probably did not care.

The second stage in the abandonment of *ákwà ọcha* is in progress in these early decades of the 21st century. Having already lost interest in producing *ákwà ọcha*, the Enuani people now seem to be losing interest in wearing it, even on culturally-significant occasions. How many times have we seen gatherings of Enuani people where hardly anybody is wearing *ákwà ọcha*? Most are decked out in Yoruba-style *agbada* and cap or in Hausa-style *babban riga*. They do look nice in the agbada attire. That is not in dispute. But that is also not the question. They would have also looked nice in three-piece Savile Row suits from London. The point here has nothing to do with looks. It has everything to do with the abandonment of your identity in favor of somebody else's. A kind of cultural colonization is in progress. But must Enuani people be consciously complicit in their own cultural colonization?

To make matters worse, even Enuani traditional rulers, the ultimate guardians of Enuani culture, are equally guilty of this abandonment. How many times do we see official gatherings of Enuani traditional rulers where most are clad in agbada or similar garbs that are borrowed from outside Enuani? Are they not aware that Enuani people look up to them to uphold Enuani culture, including their dressing culture? If the culture guardians are complicit in the abandonment of *ákwà ọcha*, what do they expect of the general populace? As Chaucer, the great poet, asked: If gold rust, what then will iron do?

The abandonment of *ákwà ọcha* is probably symptomatic of the general decay and neglect infesting Enuani culture. Hopefully, this treatise will serve as a clarion wake-up call alerting Enuani people to the endangered status of their supposedly beloved *ákwà ọcha*. Hopefully too, there will be a rallying to uphold this and other unique aspects of Enuani culture. According to the Enuani saying, if you decline to lick your lips to protect them from the dry harmattan wind, who do you expect to lick your lips for you? *Ma onye alachana mgbemgbe ọnụa, onye jeko alachalị a ya?* If Enuani people fail to patronize the *ákwà ọcha* that has been part of their age-old cultural identity, and fail to preserve their culture generally, who do they expect to uphold their culture for them?

☼ Chapter 6

Food, Farming And Famine In Enuani

Context

Every human culture has food at its foundation. Disrupt the food system, and the culture comes tumbling down. You are what you eat, so the saying goes. Given the human biological need for food, the success or failure of the food system determines how much time is available for other pursuits such as arts and recreation. The saying can therefore be expanded to indicate that a people's farming and food systems are major determinants of their nature and culture. This is definitely true of Enuani people.

The age-old food and farming systems in Enuani have changed significantly under the influence of colonialism and modernity. What we describe here is the traditional situation that existed for centuries prior to colonial contact. As such, much of the description is rendered in the past tense, even though we retain the present tense for the many aspects that remain valid into the 21st century. Several aspects have indeed changed, and we will make an effort to point out some of them. It should also be noted that the situation in some parts of Enuani may have differed slightly from what is described here.

Farming System

The Enuani farming system was strictly slash and burn, with shifting cultivation and intercropping. The farming season started towards the end of the dry season, around February or March. The first task was to identify a patch of forested land that would be the location of the farm. In order to select as virgin a forest as possible, the main farm (*ugbo ukwu*) was usually located one or two miles from the village. In addition, some farmers had a smaller supplementary farm (*egbeni*) located closer to the village.

Shifting Cultivation

Once the forested plot had been selected, slashing of the forest commenced, using machetes and axes. This clearing activity included detailed exploitation of the forest for mushrooms, snails, honey, firewood, timber, ropes, and animal game.

After slashing, the resulting debris was left in place and allowed to dry for a few weeks. The entire plot was then set on fire and allowed to burn as thoroughly as possible. The farmer spent the next couple of weeks clearing away the solid debris left after the fire (*ikpa agala*). The farm was then ready to receive the first crops.

Mushrooms

Usually, the first crops to be planted were corn (maize) and *egusi* melon (also called *ogili*). These were followed days later by yam, pumpkins, and okra/ vegetables, all intercropped on the same piece of land. The yam referred to here (and throughout this book) is the true yam, *Dioscorea* species, not the kind of sweet potato that is called Yam in some parts of the world.

Weeding, usually with machetes, was the predominant activity after planting was done. When the yams began to trail, stout stakes were sourced from nearby forests to support the yams. Native beans (*àkpáká or àkpáká ihehee*), which also required climbing support, were then planted to utilize the same stakes as the yams. Cassava was usually planted late in the season, intended for harvest the following year.

In traditional Enuani, farming was mostly done by the men, while the women were most prominent in processing, storage and marketing of the produce. It is significant that Enuani markets and market affairs were under the jurisdiction of a woman, the *Ọmụ*. She, with her council, was also recognized generally as the leader in women's affairs.

The first items to be harvested from the new farm were usually the vegetables. *Egusi* melon matured in about three months, but required extensive processing both on and off the farm. Fresh corn was also ready by June or July. Yam harvesting started around August, and continued intermittently for the rest of the farming year.

The Produce: Feast and Famine

In all of Enuani, yam held the pride of place as the noble crop. It featured prominently in the food system and in cultural matters. To the exclusion of all other crops in the Enuani food basket, yam had a whole series of religious and cultural trappings related to it. For starters, yam had its own god in traditional religion. The deity was called *Fejokwu (or Ifejokwu or Ahiajokwu)*. Foolish was the traditional farmer who did not precede the planting season for yam with propitiation to *Fejokwu*, imploring the god for a good season and an abundant harvest. Ignore *Fejokwu* and *Fejokwu* would ignore you. And your farm. And your family members. Find favor with *Fejokwu* and all would be well.

Yam in Enuani Farm

All activities throughout the farming season were geared towards producing a bumper crop of yam. The emphasis was on producing large tubers, some of which could be up to a yard in length. Even the harvesting of yam had its own attendant rituals. True traditionalists recited a small incantation as each huge tuber was pulled from the ground. As soon as the tuber was harvested, a machete was used to make a mark on it to indicate its owner. Each farmer had his own unique yam mark. Such was the degree of adulation and respect with which farmers regarded the yam. An abundant yam harvest was an indicator of wealth and prestige in the village, irrespective of how little or how much of other crops the farmer produced. One of the proudest accolades a man could bear in the village was *diji*, master of the yam. Village obligations, formal visits, dowry payments, and communal fines invariably included a stipulated number of large yam tubers. Yam was some sort of unspoken currency for denominating value. No other food crop in Enuani culture commanded such respect and attention.

By tradition, nobody was supposed to harvest their yam until the communally agreed *iwa ji* (New-Yam festival) day. New yams were forbidden to be brought to market until this day, even if some families secretly ate new yams in their homes. On the festival day, there was feasting and celebration throughout the village, with new yams featuring prominently on the menu. With time, the churches co-opted the new-yam festivals that had been in Enuani tradition for centuries before colonialism and Christianity. A date for the new-yam festival began to feature on the church calendar. The date was usually different from that for the traditional festival, to distance it from the animist offerings that accompanied the traditional festival. On the church's new-yam day, newly harvested yams were brought to church for blessing, before being taken home for the feast.

For most of Enuani, food supply ranged from ample in the months shortly after harvest (*udu-nni*), to scarce in the months preceding harvest (*unwu,* or famine). *Udu-nni* lasted approximately from July to January, while famine lasted from January through June. During the season of plenty, the main staple was yam, supplemented by maize and vegetables in various forms. It was not unusual for yam to feature in all the three meals of the day: roasted yam plus leftovers in the morning; boiled yam and vegetables in the afternoon; and pounded yam fufu with soup in the evening.

But yam as an agricultural commodity was notorious for its poor storage life. Losses in storage, mostly due to rots, could sometimes eat up more than half of the harvested crop. The bounty which *Fejǫkwụ* graciously delivered, succumbed all too readily to the degradative spell of evil gods. Consequently, by the fourth month after harvest, yam became scarce, ushering in the famine season.

The famine season was usually characterized by a more diverse diet, with less of yam and more of other commodities. For most of Enuani history, the famine season was stark. So much so that people often foraged in the bushes for wild roots, fruits and vegetables.

During the famine period, beans became a prominent item of farm produce that was pressed into service. With their high protein content, they compensated effectively for the small quantity of animal protein (meat) that was available. There were essentially three types of beans that featured in Enuani diet. The white regular cowpea (black-eye peas, *àgwà*) was the most exotic, but few Enuani farmers grew it. The area was just too humid for it, and most of what was consumed in Enuani came from the more arid climes of northern Nigeria. Eaten more frequently in Enuani was *àkpáká ihehee* (also called *okpodudu*), a long-podded bean related to the cowpea. It was apparently introduced from Ishanland. It grew well on Enuani farms.

The third kind of beans, and by far the most indigenous to Enuani, was *àkpáká Enuani,* often simply called *àkpáká.* This was a kind of African lima bean, with a short broad pod. It was associated with agriculture in Enuani from time immemorial. It served as the crucial legume for nitrogen fixation in the farming system, something that most farming systems must have. It was also a crucial protein source in the diet.

Àkpáká Enuani beans contained poisonous prussic acid (cyanide). While this poison had the advantage of repelling insects during storage, it must be removed before human consumption. For this reason, *àkpáká* was prepared by first boiling it with a large quantity of water. This water was discarded carefully, since it was poisonous and had to be kept away from children and domestic animals. The boiling continued with a fresh batch of water which was also discarded when the beans were done. Palm oil, spices, and pieces of boiled yam were mixed in, and the meal was ready for consumption. *Àkpáká* had a bland, slightly bitter taste. But the trick was that if left for a couple of days, the *àkpáká* preparation fermented and acquired a pleasant sour taste.

Processing and storage of the three kinds of beans were relatively easy. For *àkpáká ihehee* and *àkpáká Enuani*, harvesting occurred early in the dry season, around November. The heaped pods were sundried for a few days, and then shelled. The beans were then stored in large calabashes and kept on a bamboo platform (*àkpátá*) over the kitchen fireplace. The same platform held other gourds containing dry *egusi* melon seeds, dry maize, and dry castor beans. Sheaves of husk-covered maize, earmarked for the next season's planting, also passed the dry season hung over the kitchen fireplace. The *àkpátá* was a rich storehouse for anything that needed to stay dry in storage.

Cassava

One of the major sources of relief from famine in Enuani has been the arrival of cassava. Given the 21st century realities, it is hard to believe that cassava was unknown in most of Enuani as recently as the early part of the 20th century. While yam has been grown by Enuani people for millennia, and has permeated their culture, cassava was a newcomer. The arrival of cassava was very fortunate and just in time. The historical yam-based food system in Enuani was beginning to struggle under the combined onslaught of diminishing soil fertility, costly production systems, and the ravages of storage rots. Before cassava, the famine season was desperate, driving people to go hungry for long periods, or to roam about the forests digging up wild roots. Newcomer or not, cassava was destined, within a few decades, to become a major player in the Enuani food system. Cassava was a more forgiving crop, with many advantages which yam lacked. It could yield well with fewer inputs, it could stay in live storage in the farm, and it was easy to process into dry storage forms such as *gari* or flour. With these advantages, cassava quickly ingratiated itself to become a major player in the Enuani food basket.

An even more recent arrival than cassava in the Enuani menu was rice. In the 20th century, rice moved from being an occasional festival food, to being a regular menu item. But unlike cassava, very little of it is grown in Enuani.

Tree crops formed a significant part of Enuani agriculture. By far the most useful tree crop in Enuani was the African Oil Palm tree (*Elaeis* species). Being indigenous to the area, wild palms existed all over Enuani. They were exploited where they stood, until modern times when plantations were established. Virtually every part of the tree had some use in traditional Enuani. The tree provided palm oil for cooking, palm kernel oil for medicines, lumber for building, leaves for thatching, wicker for baskets and ropes, ash for making soap, etc. But culturally speaking, by far the most significant product from the oil palm tree was palm wine. This was the beverage of choice in Enuani for traditional ceremonies and general hospitality. Palm wine was essentially the sap that was tapped from the oil palm tree. Natural yeasts from the air fermented this sugary sap, imparting an alcoholic content to it.

An equally significant tree crop in Enuani culture was the kolanut tree (*Cola* species). The kolanut from the tree was the most significant item in Enuani hospitality. Paired with palm wine, as was done frequently, kolanut was the ultimate cultural totem of the Enuani people. It was what hosts presented to guests, and what people used to discharge significant obligations. So, the culturally most significant products from crops in Enuani were yam, kolanut, and palm wine.

Throughout the year, Enuani main meals were supplemented with a steady stream of fruits and nuts. These were not eaten as dessert in conjunction with meals. Instead, they were eaten at random, as snacks. The cultivated fruits, mostly seasonal, included oranges, coconuts, mango, palm fruits/nuts, banana, *ube* (African pear, *Dacryodes* species), *ugili* (*Irvingia* species), *mmịmị* (pepper fruit), *ụdala* (African star apple), groundnuts (peanuts), cashew, and pineapple. These were mostly planted around the family compound, along with plantains and cocoyams. For the children, there was also a frequent, though irregular, stream of wild forest fruits (such as *ụtụ,* and *icheku* [velvet tamarind]) that the adults chanced upon in the bush and brought home. These were special treats which the children enjoyed immensely.

Apart from wild fruits, there was a large array of small animal treats which the adults disdained, but which children enjoyed. In this category were at least four kinds of insects. First, and most abundant when in season, were the large species of termites. The children caught the termites when they flocked in large numbers for their nuptial flights, toasted them in pots, and found them very delicious. The second kind of insect was the large African cricket (*abụzụ*). These measured 2-3 inches in length and had a shrill cry which attracted mates (and children) to their burrows. The third kind of insect children ate was the yam beetle (*ébé*). These were pests on the yam crop, since they made unsightly holes in the tubers. Farmers hunted them avidly as a pest, but brought home their catch for children to enjoy. The final group of insects that children ate was the palm wine beetle (*nza ozu*). These large dark beetles with long snouts usually occurred near places where palm wine was being tapped.

Some cultures around the world may shrink at the thought of eating insects, just as Enuani persons shudder to think that some cultures eat frogs as delicacies. But, come to think of it, isn't honey one of the most delicious and most valued food items in all human societies? Is honey not, after all, the predigested regurgitate ("vomit") of a kind of insect?

In addition to fruits, adults wandering in the forest often came home with mushrooms and snails. The snails were considered as a special delicacy. The large species was the giant African snail, which could weigh over a pound. It was treated as a serious commodity, and was used in preparing the main meals. However, the smaller species (*okokolo*) was consigned to the status of a snacking commodity for the children. Children roasted them directly in the fire and ate them.

So, while children in the cities and in later generations were treated to candy and prepared snacks, village kids in traditional Enuani did not lack for snacks in the form of a steady stream of nutritious natural commodities. As with city children, these snacks flowed through the adults, and formed an important social bonding mechanism between children and adults. Many social contracts between the adults and children were written in the currency of these snacks.

Animal Husbandry

Animal husbandry took a back seat to crop production in traditional Enuani society. The little meat that featured in the diet came mostly from wild game (bush meat), hunted or trapped. On average, each family owned a few chicken, fewer goats and sheep, and still fewer pigs. Special breeds of cows that were resistant to tsetse fly existed in a few Enuani communities, but the numbers have diminished with time. All the animals were kept for meat or eggs. There was no dairying.

All the animals were free-roaming, causing frequent disputes as a result of animal trespassing or damage. A significant cultural aspect was that domestic animals were used to meet obligations or to foster relationships. Typically, one family would offer another family a young female goat to "keep". The understanding was that progeny from the goat would be shared equally by the two families. Meanwhile, the existence of the goat was a constant reminder of the inter-familial bond. Culturally, too, goats were preferred to any other kind of livestock for events such as animal sacrifices, obligations, fines, or dowry.

Some unique Enuani foods

Pounded yam: The most frequently consumed food item in traditional Enuani was pounded yam. This was made by boiling peeled yam and pounding it into a fufu dough in a mortar. The fufu was eaten by dipping morsels in a sauce ("soup") and swallowing without chewing. As a variant, the fufu dough could be made from plantains, cassava, cocoyams, or a mixture of these with yam in varying proportions.

Cocoyam

"Soup": The soup for the fufu can be grouped generally into four kinds.

1.   Draw soup which was slimy. The main ones were *Agbọnọ (Irvingia* species*)*, *Ọkwụlụ* (okra) and *Ujuju*.

2.   Non-draw oil soup: The most popular in this group by far was *Egusi* soup, which usually had palm oil in it. *Onugbu* (bitterleaf, *Vernonia* species) was the favorite green vegetable for *egusi* soup. Non-draw oil soups also included *ofe akwụ*,

where the palm oil was replaced by the extracts from fresh oil-palm fruits.

Egusi

3.   *Nsala*: This kind of soup, usually cooked without oil, was said to serve a semi-medicinal purpose. It was often cooked for people who were unwell or in post-partum recovery. *Nsala* was usually very spicy, and is sometimes rendered in English as "pepper soup". The significant ingredients for *nsala* included *Ụtazịzị* leaf, *Ụzịza* (a kind of black pepper), *Ụda* dry fruit, *Ehulu* seeds, or the roots/bark of trees such as *Osumade* and *Tamakpa*.

4.   *Ose anị*: This was a rare kind of soup, usually prepared by grinding the mixed ingredients in the flat wooden mortar (*mkpilite*), without boiling them together. The significant ingredients could be the same as the other kinds of soup listed above. The main difference was in the mode of preparation. Some ingredients, such as *egusi*, okra, or *ujuju*, needed to be toasted or boiled slightly, before joining the other ingredients in the *mkpilite*.

Roasted or boiled yam/plantain/cocoyam: Yam, plantain, or cocoyam, roasted over a fire or boiled, was eaten with palm oil. As a variant, the oil, vegetables and spices were added to the peeled yam/plantain/cocoyam during boiling to produce a kind of pottage called *awaị*. In Enuani, cassava was never eaten boiled or roasted, mainly because the cassava varieties present contained poisonous prussic acid (cyanide) which must be removed through processing.

Roasted or boiled corn with *ube* or coconut: Fresh corn and *ube* came into season at about the same time, and were often eaten together.

Ụkpọ: This is a kind of dumpling, somewhat akin to the Mexican tamale. The starchy ingredient was yam, fresh corn, or plantain. The mashed up ingredient was mixed with palm oil, spices and maybe pieces of fish. Portions were wrapped in *Ụma* leaves or plantain leaves, and then steamed. The resulting product was *ụkpọ ji* (from yam), *ụkpọ ọgẹdẹ* (from plantain), or *ụkpọ ọka* (from corn). A similar product made from beans (cowpea) was called *ọlẹlẹ* or *mai-mai* (*moin moin*).

Oli and *agidi*: These two items were made from ground dry corn. For *agidi*, the extracted corn starch was thickened over a fire. Portions were then scooped onto *Ụma* or plantain leaves and wrapped. It was consumed by itself or with soup. *Oli* was made in a similar way, but had more of the corn chaff in it, and came out firmer in texture. It was more chewy than *agidi*, and could keep for a longer time.

Àkpáká: The preparation and consumption of *àkpáká* beans has already been described above.

Àkàlà: This was a kind of fritter made by frying batter in palm oil. Historically, the batter was made from dry corn (for *àkàlà ọka*) or from water yam (for *àkàlà ji mbọ*). More and more frequently in recent times, the batter came to be made from beans (cowpea), and the product was simply called *àkàlà*. [This product was called *àkàrà* in other parts of the country, but many Enuani subdialects lack the "r" sound].

Àkàlà (Àkàrà)

The use of tobacco was fairly common in traditional Enuani. The tobacco was used in pipes by men and elderly women, while some of it was ground up for snuff. Cigarettes and cigars were unknown in traditional Enuani society, and only arrived more recently.

Much of the tobacco used in traditional Enuani came from other parts of the country, since very little tobacco was grown in Enuani. However, there was a variety of tobacco that was grown sporadically in Enuani. This tobacco was used for *ukòkò*. *Ukòkò* was a huge pipe, very much resembling the famous Swiss alphorn, except that the part sitting on the ground was the combustion chamber. This combustion chamber was made of clay pottery material. From the chamber, a hollow wooden pipe, some 3-4 feet long, channeled the smoke to the smoker who sat on a chair.

Ofi (Ụgụ)

A common snack item in traditional Enuani was *akó* (or *ẹkó*), a hard grayish clay material that was sourced from stream banks. *Akó* had a pleasant taste when bits of it were allowed to dissolve in the mouth just like candy. Alternatively, *akó* was ground up with water and some salt, molded into pellets, dried, and eaten as a snack candy. *Akó* was mostly eaten for its taste, even though modern research has suggested possible health benefits of some edible clays.

There exist numerous other unique Enuani foods (e.g. *Ụgbaà* [oilbean], *Ụkwa, Ofi/Ụgụ,* etc.), in addition to numerous snack items (e.g. *Mmịmị, Ụkpa*). As indicated earlier, cassava and rice are of more recent emergence in Enuani, and have not been included in this list. In general, the fortunes of each kind of food wax or wane depending on the locality or the era.

☼ Chapter 7

Enuani Mother Tongue Is
An Endangered Species

Why and how do languages suddenly die? How would you like your generation to be the last one to speak your language? All over the world, the phenomenon of language *abandonment* at the family level is precipitating a crisis of language *extinction* at the community level. From India to the Americas, from the Congo basin to Papua New Guinea, from Indonesia to Nigeria, many indigenous languages are being lost due to neglect, worsened by the insidious intrusion of the world's major languages. Just as species extinction deprives the world of its biological heritage, language extinction abrasively erodes the world's cultural heritage. The genesis of this erosion lies within individual families. The seeds of decay lie secretly buried in the home.

To the casual observer, Enuani language is alive and thriving, at least within the Enuani geographical area. But closer examination reveals huge cracks that suggest that all is not well. Enuani language, while not dead, is currently on life support. It is in the inglorious company of hundreds of global languages that are threatened by abandonment and eventual extinction. We'll use Enuani language here as a case study of how and why languages attenuate and eventually die.

Let's say you're living in New York. You are an indigene of the Enuani ethnic group in Nigeria, and you are proud of it. Congratulations! Your spouse, too, is from Enuani. Congratulations again. Before you came over to the U.S.A., you resided in Lagos, outside the Enuani ethnic area, and all your four children were born in Lagos. During those years in Lagos, and up till now, your family's language in the home ("home language") has been English. Now, none of your children can speak your Enuani language. Their mates at school do not even believe them when they say they are from Enuani, since they cannot back up the claim with the required language skills. So, wherein lies their claim to being Enuani indigenes? Where have they failed? Where have you failed in your parenting?

No, you have not failed; at least judging from the fact that you've got plenty of company. Many other parents in the US and within Nigeria are in the same awkward position. So, too, are parents from many other countries around the world who find that they have failed to pass on their native language to their children. To their eternal embarrassment, they find that they are the last generation in their line to speak the language. They have given birth to linguistic eunuchs, stranded in a linguistic dead-end.

Let's use the Enuani/Nigerian parents as an example, since their situation has similarities in many other countries around the world. It is amazing these days to observe the number of Nigerian families that use English as the means of communication within the home (i.e. the home language). This is particularly so among the middle and upper class families, who sometimes give the impression that their claim to modernity is reinforced by the use of English as the home language. Part of this attitude is a vestige of the colonial era, when elite boarding schools promoted the use of English on campus, and indeed punished students who spoke any of the local languages at school. While this was a well-meaning accommodation for students of diverse linguistic backgrounds, it unconsciously promoted the impression that English was superior to any of the indigenous languages.

The position of the English language in Nigerian officialdom is clear and unassailable. It is the one official language that permits communication between the various parts and segments of the multi-ethnic multi-lingual country. In most urban centers, with their mix of various ethnic/linguistic groups, the English language (or adaptations from it) also serves as the common medium of expression on the street. The use of English to communicate among persons with different mother tongues is certainly borne out of necessity. Its use in these circumstances can be said to be obligatory. In contrast, the use of English within the home is very often elective, especially in situations where both parents originate from the same linguistic group. The elective use of English within the home exists in virtually all ethnic groups in the country. It is only for purposes of illustration that this discussion focuses on the Enuani people. Otherwise, the discussion is just as applicable to other ethnic and linguistic groups in Nigeria, and even in the world generally.

Let's start by considering the simplest situation where husband and wife are both from Enuani, and the children, by derivation, are also Enuani indigenes (i.e. the family is mono-ethnic). There is a commonality of origin and language for the entire family. It is surprising that even in such a situation, many families can be found using English as the home language. Surely, there is a crass incongruity in a situation where father, mother, and children collectively conspire to abandon their common linguistic heritage, and opt to communicate with one another in a tongue that is alien to every one of them. One would have to search quite hard to find a Japanese man married to a Japanese woman of the same linguistic extraction, adopting some other language for intra-familial communication. The same could be said of Germans, Tongans, Vietnamese, Russians, and many other ethnic groups around the world. But in Enuani, in Nigeria, and in many post-colonial societies, the situation is different.

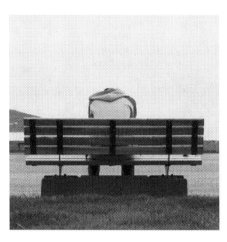

Now, let's take an analytical look at how a nuclear family adopts and entrenches the home language (be it their mother tongue or English or any other language). The seeds of the pattern are sown very early in the life of the nuclear family, usually when the couple are still alone and the children are yet to arrive. If the spouses communicate with each other in their mother tongue, they are able to initiate the first child/dependent into the practice. In our example, a critical mass of Enuani speakers would have been formed. Subsequent additions to the family (children or wards) simply follow the existing pattern, and unwittingly enlarge the pool of Enuani speakers. Soon, the presence of the parents is no longer necessary for the children to continue using the mother tongue within the home. The mother tongue has become the home language.

As the group enlarges, it gathers a momentum of its own, and the home language becomes entrenched and self-perpetuating. Dislodging the entrenched home language to substitute another becomes progressively more difficult as time goes on and the family group enlarges. Once the home linguistic compass is set early in one direction, it becomes difficult to re-set in another direction. So, whether it is the mother tongue, English, or any other language that takes hold as the home language early in the life of the family, making a change later on may prove extremely difficult. So, if you want Enuani to be your home language, you must introduce it early. That's the key.

The language of communication between husband and wife in the early stages of marriage is therefore critical in determining the life-long home language of the family. This also reveals how the adoption of English as the home language comes about in many mono-ethnic Nigerian families. One of the spouses, perhaps lacking adequate grounding in their mother tongue, may be more comfortable communicating in English in the home. The other spouse obliges, eager not to offend. Then the first child obliges; subsequent children oblige; wards and live-in relatives oblige. The stage is now set for life-long use of English as the home language, producing a generation of children that are effectively shut out from their supposed mother tongue.

In most instances, the use of English as the home language is not arrived at by deliberate reasoned choice. It simply comes about by default, but is permitted or tolerated by the family members. There is little or no conscious evaluation of the relative advantages of using English as opposed to the mother tongue as the home language. Such a cavalier attitude to choosing the home language presupposes that there are no far-reaching consequences of choosing English instead of the mother tongue to serve as the home language. The risks implicit in this assumption will be addressed later.

Even in cases where the nuclear family is ostensibly mono-ethnic and mono-linguistic, ethnic pluralism can come through the influence of nannies or child-minders. If the child-minder, whether resident or part-time, is of a different linguistic extraction from the rest of the family, she invariably communicates with the child in the home in English. This establishes a beach-head for the promotion of English as the home language. Everybody else in the family is obliged to communicate with the child-minder in English, and vice versa. If the child-minder is of the full-time live-in type, there is a heightened frequency and intensity of this inevitable communication in English in the home. The beach-head for English as the home language is thus enlarged significantly, while the family's mother tongue is progressively occluded. The family is now in a dilemma: either operate in two different languages (i.e. English and the mother tongue), or take the easy way out and use English alone as the home language. As implied already, the second option is the easier one, and many families choose it uncritically. Only a few families are able to insist on retaining the mother tongue. However, achieving this depends on the willingness and ability of the parents to spend a good proportion of their time with the children. This requirement cannot easily be met by many working executive parents. They just cannot match the long hours that the child-minder spends with the child each day, all the time communicating in English. The child-minder is, therefore, a very potent influence in pushing the family towards the adoption of English as the home language. Her influence can, in fact, subvert and subdue the initial efforts of the young couple to retain their mother tongue as the home language.

The adoption of English as the home language can, therefore, arise from one spouse being uncomfortable with the mother tongue, or from the insidious influence of a child-minder who hails from another linguistic group. A third predisposing situation for the mono-ethnic nuclear family is where such a family lives outside their own linguistic area. This could be within the same country (e.g. the Enuani indigene living in Lagos), or in another country. In such cases, English is the language of communication for the children at school and on the street (including when they are at play with the neighborhood children). Such a large part of their day is spent communicating in English that its importation into the home to serve as the home language is only a matter of time. Such pressures are particularly strong in cosmopolitan multi-ethnic cities such as Warri, Lagos, Port Harcourt, or Jos, where a form of English is the language on the street. Similar pressures also exist for mono-ethnic families living overseas (e.g. the Enuani indigenes living in New York or London). Parents in such families require a tremendous amount of effort if they desire to ward off the encroachment of English into the home.

For the truly mono-ethnic Enuani family, one argument often heard in favor of English as the home language runs like this: Since English is the country's lingua franca, its use at home (as well as in school) enhances the child's proficiency in it. Even if this argument is valid, one may ask: at what cost is this additional proficiency being achieved? If the child speaks English at school, and also English in the home, where, one may ask, is he supposed to acquire proficiency in his mother tongue? This question is particularly poignant for the child living outside his native linguistic area (in-country or overseas), since English may also be the language of the street, in addition to being that of school and home.

Proficiency in English is a worthy goal. But so also is proficiency in the mother tongue. The achievement of one must not be at the expense of the other. Indeed, social anthropologists tell us that language is not just a means of communication. It also influences our thought processes, our world view, and our cultural perspective. Our mother tongue is, therefore, more than a means of communicating with others; it is a condensed package of our cultural being. It is our most significant identity symbol to prove our membership of our claimed ethnic group. Therefore, a child who is denied proficiency in his mother tongue is simultaneously denied an important aspect of the culture of his people. Some would go so far as to assert that proficiency in the mother tongue is an inalienable right of every child, and is indispensable for his normal cultural development. A parent who denies the child this right is inflicting insidious harm.

Once we are convinced of the need for the child to acquire proficiency in his mother tongue, we must ensure that the opportunity for such acquisition is presented. There is no better place for the child to acquire and practice his mother tongue than in his primary support group, the family. This acquisition starts long before formal schooling commences. Indeed, one can argue that the child will have ample opportunity to learn and practice English at school later. In contrast, the mother tongue that fails to be presented to the child at home may never again be adequately presented to him all through his life.

The danger inherent in producing children who are not well grounded in their mother tongue should not be underestimated. Such children grow up to be adults with dubious cultural identity. Neither here nor there. They are sentenced to a lifetime of apologies and excuses. Just imagine the offspring's embarrassment when he has to make excuses like, "My parents and I are from Enuani, but I can't speak the language." The excuse is just as awkward in groups of Enuani people, as it is in groups of mixed ethnicities where most people assume you can speak Enuani once you say you are an Enuani indigene. And imagine how many times in his life he has to go through such embarrassment, all because his parents failed to present his mother tongue as his home language.

It gets worse. Such an adult eventually gets married and feels very uncomfortable conversing with his spouse in the mother tongue. As already explained, this is a major predisposing factor pressuring the obliging family to slide towards English as the home language. The children growing up in the new family, in turn, will be poorly grounded in the mother tongue; and so on. The attenuation of the mother tongue in the home continues through succeeding generations, until the mother tongue is completely lost. Completely extinguished in that lineage.

Poor grounding in the mother tongue is thus self-perpetuating through the generations of families, until we find that at the community level, a sizeable fraction of the ethnic group cannot even speak the language that identifies them. They are unable to show the prima facie identity card (language proficiency) to back up their claim to membership of Enuani or other ethnic group. How can you convince me that you are Yoruba when you cannot speak Yoruba? How do you assert that you are Efik, if you cannot speak Efik? The same with Enuani. Such claim to membership of an ethnic group, without speaking the language, can only be nominal and, in all sincerity, spurious.

For the mono-ethnic family living outside its indigenous linguistic area (but still within Nigeria), the child is sometimes faced with learning or using three languages at the same time: one for school (English), one for the street, and one for the home. For example, an Enuani child living in Calabar would have to juggle English in school, Efik on the street, and Enuani at home. Some families think that this is too much for the child, and justify using English at home so that the child only has to cope with two languages. This resolution to the problem underrates the considerable capacity of young children to learn several languages simultaneously, and to switch back and forth as the situation demands. Let us now examine why this solution must be considered facile.

The importance of the mother tongue for the child is in no way diminished by his living outside his indigenous linguistic area. If anything, the mother tongue in this case takes on added significance in at least two ways. First, the child living within his indigenous linguistic area has some opportunity to practice and use his mother tongue on the street. The Enuani child living in Ogwashi-Uku is inundated with the Enuani language once he steps out the door. Even if his parents don't speak Enuani to him within the home, there's plenty of it on the street. In contrast, the same Enuani child living at Ibadan (outside his linguistic area) cannot get Enuani exposure on the street. Any child living outside his linguistic area is denied exposure to his mother tongue on the street. His only meaningful contact with his mother tongue must be within the home. If the mother tongue is not available in the home, then it is not available at all. Therefore, the need to offer the mother tongue in the home is more imperative in this circumstance of living outside the linguistic area, even though paradoxically the pressure to install English as the home language is greater (as explained earlier).

Secondly, the child growing up outside his indigenous linguistic area is geographically distanced from and denied most of the cultural activities of his own people. The community cultural festivals, rituals, rites of passage, initiation rites, traditional ceremonies, etc. are usually performed within the geographical confines of his linguistic group. The Enuani child living in Ogwashi-Uku can observe Enuani cultural events week after week, to his heart's content. He can even participate in some of them. By contrast, an Enuani child living in Ibadan, Calabar, Lagos or New York is unable to observe the title-taking ceremonies, or new-yam festivals, or the bride-taking *ibu mmanya,* that are a regular part of life within Enuani. By the sheer dictates of geography, he is denied many of the trappings of his indigenous culture. But this culture-starved child can access the one aspect of culture that overrides the strictures of geography. That aspect is language. Language is, in a way, a portable aspect of culture. The child and his parents can indulge in it freely wherever they live, even outside the geographical confines of their indigenous linguistic area. If it's not made available to the child living outside his linguistic area, then the cultural starvation of the child is complete.

So, of all the facets of his native culture, the mother tongue is perhaps the most readily available to the child living outside his indigenous linguistic area. If the child is now denied even this little aspect of his culture, then he grows up in a total cultural vacuum, since he is already denied most other aspects of his culture because of distance. Just like fast food in the modern era, the mother tongue is a take-out slice of the indigenous culture, which the family can take wherever they go. Like the fast-food take-out, it may not offer all the ingredients for nourishment, but it can stave off cultural starvation in the interim. The mother tongue, then, is a slice of Enuani culture that is readily available to the Enuani child growing up in Lagos, Calabar, or Koton Karfi; or for that matter, in Chicago, Manila, Harare, Istanbul, or Santiago de Chile. No other slice of his culture is so globally accessible. No other slice is so globally portable. No child should be denied even this thin slice by parents who fail to present it.

For the family living outside its linguistic area, there is one additional, albeit peripheral, advantage to using the mother tongue. The use of the mother tongue by family members fosters a sense of belonging, cohesion, and exclusivity. The Enuani family in New York can carry on a spirited mother-tongue conversation in a public place without the risk of losing the confidentiality of their communication. It is as if they have access to a dedicated channel of communication that is not accessible to their neighbors. The family feels as one in their ability to use this channel. The ability to use the mother tongue inspires in them much greater internal solidarity than if they could only communicate in the language used by everybody else around. Such a family also attracts a greater degree of authenticity to its claim that it has its origins in Enuani.

We see that for the mono-ethnic family, there is a strong temptation to have English as the home language when the family lives outside its indigenous linguistic area. Yet, it is precisely such a family that most desperately needs to have the mother tongue as the home language. This is because the child has fewer casual opportunities to acquire the mother tongue or to indulge in other aspects of his indigenous culture.

While the mono-ethnic family can maintain its mother tongue as the home language by sheer will and unanimity, the situation is infinitely more complex for multi-ethnic families, where husband and wife hail from different linguistic groups. Such couples usually communicate with each other in English (or other lingua franca). The language question is either never addressed, or is allowed to take care of itself. In this situation, English offers itself least contentiously as the home lingua franca. Multi-ethnicity of the marriage is, therefore, a very strong pre-disposing factor for English to emerge as the home language. The children grow up being proficient in English alone, and are unable to speak the language of either parent. This solution is the easiest to implement, even though it is culturally the least commendable. It is like a dog-in-the-manger situation where each spouse, rather than concede to the other, prefers that neither of their mother tongues should be the home language of the family.

A more desirable option, for the sake of the children, could be for the family to adopt the language of one of the spouses as the home language. The actual choice of whose language should be adopted will be governed by the cultural expectations of the spouses, the language of the surrounding community, gender chauvinism, and whether one spouse already speaks the other spouse's language.

Then there is the very peculiar situation in which one of the spouses already has English (in any of its forms world-wide) as his or her mother tongue. In that case, the choice is between introducing the language of the other spouse, or letting the family carry on with English as its only home language.

In summary, does it really matter if the Enuani family adopts English as its home language? Are there any disadvantages in adopting English, instead of the mother tongue, as the home language? As already emphasized, the mother tongue is of such crucial importance to a child's sense of identity that its acquisition should not be left to chance. A casual approach to the question by many individuals has already led to the use of English as the home language in an alarming number of families in Nigeria and globally. This has progressively led to the production of hordes of cultural misfits who, having long lost contact with their indigenous culture in deed, are now losing it in word as well. Worse still, such individuals tend to propagate the malady by generating mostly their own kind.

It is important to remember that everybody's circumstance is different. We also differ in terms of our degree of commitment to language preservation and propagation. Courtesy demands that we refrain from being judgmental about how each person or family has addressed this issue. However, there is something commendable about each family having a deliberate policy that permits the child to acquire and use his mother tongue. The easiest way of achieving this is to entrench the mother tongue as the language for daily communication within the home. This is particularly important for the family sojourning in alien or foreign lands. In such cases, the mother tongue serves as a portable and readily-available parcel of the home culture, while at the same time enhancing family cohesion and authenticity.

The larger issue of preserving the communal/global cultural heritage also dictates that the mother tongue should not be abandoned. The seeds of the world-wide scourge of language extinction arise insidiously in each family that fails to pass on its language to its children. Unfortunately, Enuani language, like many others around the world, is not immune to the threats of language abandonment and extinction. The mother tongue is like the roof of your home in the Enuani proverb, *Be onye bi ka ọ wachi.* If you do not mend and maintain the roof over your own home, who do you expect to do it for you? Nobody else will.

☼ SECTION III ☼

Enuani Proverbs:
Window On Enuani
Culture [Atụtụ Inu]

☼ Chapter 8

Dissecting Enuani Proverbs

Rich language diversity in Enuani

You could well nominate Enuani language for a world prize in terms of diversity. And your nominee just might win. Very few languages in the world can match Enuani in this respect. Enuani language embraces a very rich diversity of sub-dialects, which differ from town to town and from hamlet to hamlet. Virtually every town or hamlet has its own distinguishable sub-dialect. As an example, let's take the rural towns of Ukala-Okpuno, Onicha-Olona, and Akwukwu-Igbo. These three towns form a triangle, and each one shares a boundary with the other two. This means that the distance from one town to the other is technically zero, and the distance of habitations from one to the other is a fraction of a mile. Yet, each of these three towns has its own distinguishable sub-dialect of Enuani. Similarly, contiguous towns like Ubulu-Ukwu, Ogwasi-Uku, Igbuzo (Ibusa) and Asaba each have their distinguishable sub-dialects. A keen listener can tell what town an Enuani person comes from simply by the spoken sub-dialect.

With such a rich diversity of sub-dialects, rendering pan-Enuani proverbs presents quite a challenge. Which sub-dialect do you use? What we have tried to do is to present the proverbs in an Enuani rendering that is intelligible to all Enuani persons, dispensing with the peculiar idiosyncrasies that occur in the various sub-dialects. The core meaning of each proverb occurs in all of Enuani, even though each town might render it in its own peculiar sub-dialect.

Pronouncing Enuani (Phonetics)

In Enuani speech, the vowel *a* is always in the short form as in *Adam*. But the vowels *e, i, o,* and *u* have both long and short forms. In addition, there are specific sounds in Enuani that are not normally encountered in English. These include *gb* as in **àgbà** (jaw); *gw* as in **àgwà** (beans); *kw* as in **àkwà** (bed); *kp* as in **àkpà** (bag); *nw* as in **ánwụ** (sun); *ny* as in **ányá** (eye).

There is a unique consonant in spoken Enuani that occurs in such words as **alịlịọ** (plea), **olili** (feast), **ọlịa** (illness), or **ulịọ** (finger snapping). This consonant sounds like an equal mixture of the sounds for the letters *l, d,* and *r*. It is often written as *l,* and some modern speakers even voice it as an *l* sound. But it is distinctly different from the pure *l* sound found in such Enuani words as **ọlụ** (work), **ilòlò** (thought), **ule** (laziness), or **ụla** (sleep). Not being experts in languages, we leave it to the expert linguists to determine the origin, prevalence, and use of this peculiar consonant. We note though that this consonant is also present in some other Igbo-related dialects outside Enuani.

Enuani language is tonal. A word spelt the same way can have several different meanings, depending on the emphasis placed or not placed on the respective syllables. The famous example is the four-letter word, *a-k-w-a,* which can mean cry (**ákwá**), cloth (**ákwà**), egg (**àkwá**), or bed (**àkwà**), depending on the pitch or tone of each of the two syllables.

Persons who desire to hear how the proverbs sound when rendered in Enuani language are encouraged to visit enuaniculture. com or enuani.com and related websites.

Writing Enuani (Orthography)

Enuani was historically not a written language. It does not have an orthography of its own. The orthography used in this work has been modified from neighboring languages and dialects, especially Igbo, Yoruba and Edo (e.g. see *The Official Igbo Orthography* as recommended by the Onwu Committee in 1961). Generally, we have used a dot (the diacritic) under the vowel to indicate the short form of the vowel, while the long form does not have the dot. Nouns and pronouns are written as stand-alone words.

Tonality is indicated by using the back *Grave* accent mark (e.g. à) to indicate a low tone or pitch, and using the forward *Acute* accent mark (e.g. á) to indicate a high tone. If we look at the earlier example of a-k-w-a, when both vowels have the backward accent it is **àkwà** (bed); but when both vowels have the forward accent we get **ákwá** (cry). And so on for other words.

In this work, as in many Enuani writings, we have used the tonal accent marks sparingly. Using them for every word would be overwhelming. So, we have used them only in situations where their absence would lead to ambiguity. In other cases, we hope that the context will indicate the meaning and guide the pronunciation.

In casual writing, people sometimes ignore both the vowel dots and the tonal accent marks.

Strict linguists may spot errors here and there in the orthography that we have used, but we believe we have made ourselves sufficiently understood.

Table: Guide to Pronouncing and Writing Enuani

Following from the preceding sections, below is a more detailed summary guide on pronouncing and writing Enuani.

Symbol	Enuani as in...	English sound approx.	Comment
a	**afa** ...name	A̱bout	
e	**ene** ...deer	A̱ble	
ẹ	**ẹfẹ** ...dress	Dre̱ss	
i	**isi** ...head	E̱ven	
ị	**apịtị** ...mud	Pi̱ty	
o	**olome** ...orange	O̱pen	
ọ	**ọka** ...corn	co̱rn	
u	**ube** ...native pear	so̱o̱n, fo̱o̱l	
ụ	**ụsụ** ...bat	fu̱ll	
ṇ	**eṇe** ...verdict	ha̱ṉger, riṉg	
`(Grave accent mark)	**àkwà** ...bed		Low tonality
´(Acute accent mark)	**ákwá** ...cry		High tonality
Gw	**àgwà** ...beans	G̱wen	
Gb	**àgbà** ...jaw	Ru̱gby	
Kw	**okwu** ...speech	Q̱uick	
Kp	**àkpà** ...bag		
Nw	**anwụ** ...sun		
Ny	**ányá** ...eye		

Role and Setting of Proverbs in Enuani diction

Just like Enuani food, Enuani diction is spicy. The spice is provided by a liberal sprinkling of proverbs, parables and aphorisms. Fluent speakers in the village can hardly say more than a few sentences without punctuating their speech with a proverb for added effect. Proverbs are, therefore, a very crucial seasoning element of Enuani language.

Most of the proverbs represent lessons drawn from situations and observations of everyday life in Enuani. As such, the proverbs are vivid reflections of Enuani culture. Many of them are condensed metaphors. Since many of these proverbs crept into the language in early times, they usually echo traditional Enuani society, before the advent of colonial rule, Christianity, or other external influences. Unless specifically noted, virtually all the proverbs in this work are set in the traditional pre-colonial Enuani society.

Having said that, there remains a dynamic nature to Enuani proverbs. Some die out due to disuse or changed circumstances, while new ones arise and may become popular. A handful of proverbs listed in this work belong to this category of recent proverbs, and are identified as such. In the spirit of this dynamism, we have contributed several brand new proverbs of our own creation, and have indicated them as such in the listing. Hopefully, we have enriched Enuani lore by supplying these proverbs based on metaphors observable in Enuani society.

Apart from enriching the diction, Enuani proverbs and parables are used in other ways. Some short ones are given as person names to newborn babies, e.g. **ezí áfà ka ego** (a good name is better than riches). Others may find use as praise names adopted by notable personalities in the society. This is especially true of proverbs that break conveniently into two parts. The person doing the praising says the first part, and the person being praised completes the proverb with the second part. For example, the praiser might say,

anụ kpọ nkwụ…(the dry meat…), while the person being praised retorts, **na eju ọnụ** (fills the mouth).

Enuani proverbs number in the thousands. What we have presented here is only a small sample. We trust that our work will spur others to undertake further detailed exploration into the rich lode of treasure represented by Enuani proverbs. Ranging farther afield, we hope that this work encourages people of other ethnicities to explore the proverbs and sayings of their own ethnic group.

Notes on the Proverb Compilation

Each proverb presented below is thoroughly examined from many angles. For each one, we present its literal translation, figurative meaning, an example of its use, and some useful comments mostly related to its cultural context. A typical Enuani man, named Awele, is used in most of the examples. The reader is encouraged to think of various other examples and contexts in which each proverb could be used.

This compilation includes a varied mix of sayings. Strictly speaking, they can be categorized as proverbs, maxims, parables, aphorisms, metaphors, or idioms. But we have chosen to use these terms interchangeably. For simplicity, we refer to them all simply as **Proverbs**. Each proverb listing is self-contained. However, we have provided the added feature of cross-referencing many of the proverbs to other proverbs that are similar. All this enhances the usefulness of the listing for reference purposes.

As a rule, the translations into English have been kept simple. However, a few cases require specific English words to bring out the full flavor of the proverb. In such cases, accuracy has prevailed over simplicity.

ANALYSIS OF THE PROVERBS
will now follow…

✿ Abụzụ gba nkịtị na-atụụ ọnụ

Literally: The cricket that stays quiet is digging a hole.

Figuratively: Quietness or silence in some people should not be mistaken for inactivity.

Example: Despite the provocations from some of his workmates over many months, Awele kept quiet and did not respond, but was carefully plotting out his response. **"Abụzụ..."**

Comment: Quiet deliberation on how to respond to a situation is sometimes more beneficial than rash rapid response.... Incidentally, the Abuzu is a large type of cricket that is sought after and eaten by Enuani children. It usually lives in its hole in the ground, and has to be dug up by the children. Abuzu is known for its shrill, loud chirp, each chirp lasting many seconds. It seems that biologically, the primary purpose of the chirp is to attract a mate to the burrow. But this chirp gives away its location to the children hunting it. Folk thinking is that in the interval between chirps, Abuzu is busy digging its burrow. Hence the saying, **Abụzụ...**

❀ Agadi adị-ata ọka akamkpolo

Literally: An old person does not eat the hard dry corn.

Figuratively: Old people should refrain from indulging in the exuberances of youth.

Example: Awele's elderly father indulged in playing football with the youth team of the town, and sustained numerous injuries as a result. Awele tried to restrain him from all the exuberance by reminding him that **Agadi...**

Comment: Enuani people have a huge respect for age. Old people are treated with a lot of deference. Reciprocally, the elderly are expected to behave in ways that are consistent with the respect accorded to them.... For consumption, the dried corn on the cob is usually roasted close to the embers of the kitchen fire. Most of the kernels do not pop, meaning that strong teeth are needed to eat the roasted corn. For older people, this is quite a challenge.

❀ Ahụ fokẹ ike ogbuẹ tụịị

Literally: The anus, casting around for what to do, utters a fart.

Figuratively: Idleness can lead to extraordinary or damaging behavior.

Example: During the nine months when Awele was jobless, he didn't know what to do with his time or himself. So he slowly slid into the habit of popping into bars and getting drunk. **Ahụ...**

Comment: The idle mind is the devil's workshop.

✿ Aka dokwama ọfịa o mẹẹ ụnọ

Literally: It is by putting in effort that you can convert a patch of forest into a built home.

Figuratively: Things that appear rough and disorganized should not be ignored, because they could blossom to high value with a little input of effort. Hard work will pay off.

Example: Years ago, Awele bought an old junky Toyota car. He worked hard on it every weekend. Now, the car is gleaming and running smoothly. It has become the envy of his comrades. **Aka...**

Comment: The diamond in the rough becomes shiny and valuable with polishing. Just as effort can transform a bush into a built home, so, conversely, can a home become a bush if abandoned or neglected. Such is the cycle of nature.

✿ Aka nni kwǫa aka ekpe, aka ekpe akwǫa aka nni

Literally: The right hand washes the left hand, and the left hand washes the right hand.

Figuratively: Mutual collaboration leads to mutual benefits.

Example: When Awele was fixing up his junky car, he received a lot of help from his cousin who was a mechanic. In turn, Awele helped his cousin to prepare and file the registration documents for his mechanic workshop. The assistance flowed both ways. **Aka nni...**

Comment: Mutual or community collaboration is highly prized in Enuani. The pooled talents of the collaborators lead to symbiotic mutual benefits for all. The whole is bigger than the sum of its parts. Traditional Enuani culture placed high value on a sense of community, as opposed to individualism. Many things, including land, forests, and streams, were communally owned.

✿ Akaine, Ahoaine

Literally: Next year and every year.

Figuratively: Happy anniversary of an event (such as a birthday, wedding, etc.); or simply, Happy New Year.

Example: When Awele woke up on New Year's Day, he went over to his father and said, **"Akaine, Ahoaine."**

Comment: This is a curt greeting that can be exchanged on birthdays and other annual occurrences.

✿ `Akwụ` fesiẹ ọ daalị áwọ`

Literally: After fluttering around, the termite ultimately falls to the ground to be eaten by the toad.

Figuratively: Do not be deceived by pretentious showiness. A reality check will ultimately restore normalcy. The proud and showy person will eventually be brought low.

Example: Awele had a hard time wooing his then girlfriend. Because of her beauty, she was hugely distracted by numerous suitors, each one showy but phony. With time, she was able to discern the

insincerity of many of these suitors. Awele's persistence and perseverance ultimately paid off. After flirting around with the others, she latched on to him. `Akwụ` fesiẹ…

Comment: What goes up must come down, if you have enough patience. All that glitters is not gold, or even golden.… Incidentally, the large flying termite is an edible insect delicacy in Enuani. During the flocking nuptial flights of the termites, people catch thousands of them, then toast them and eat them. Very delicious.

✿ ´Alá nwagbọọ da nị enwenẹ nkwọnihẹ

Literally: Once the maiden's breasts sag downward, they cannot be restored to the original position.

Figuratively: Certain things and situations turn out to be irreversible.

Example: Awele forgot to put oil in his car for a while, and the engine began to malfunction. Even though he was able to drive it to the mechanic's shop, all efforts to revive it failed. Eventually, the mechanic had to break the sad news to Awele that the engine had knocked. It was beyond repair and there was no way to bring it back to life. ´**Alá...**

Comment: This Enuani proverb obviously predated today's plastic surgery which can indeed restore the sagged breasts to their original position. Yet, many things in life remain irreversible.

✿ Amalïká na amàlïkà zụa afịa, elele ádị àdị a

Literally: When one shrewd person transacts in trade with another shrewd one, it is hard for either person to make a profit.

Figuratively: When two clever people go against each other, it's difficult for either to gain undue advantage.

Example: While his antagonistic workmate was maneuvering to get Awele fired, Awele himself was laying down his own strategy. He was able to checkmate the workmate each time the workmate made a move. They knew each other's strengths and weaknesses, and it was difficult for either of them to notch up huge advantages over the other. It was some sort of stalemate. **Amalịká...**

Comment: When two shrewd persons deny each other any undue advantage, their contest is most likely to end in a draw.

❀ Anụ kpọ nkwụ na-eju ọnụ

Literally: The hard dry meat fills the mouth.

Figuratively: The small insignificant item can turn out to be very potent.

Example: The little village boy could out-wrestle much bigger opponents. His friends took to calling him **Anụ...**

Comment: This proverb can be rendered as a statement that little things can be powerful; or as a description of a little thing that is powerful...With no electricity or refrigeration in traditional Enuani society, drying meat was the only effective way to preserve it. It shrank in size during drying, but swelled to its full size when the dry meat was being chewed in the mouth.

✿ Anụmanụ nchá na-achọ àkwụ̀ olili

Literally: All animals find the winged termite as a delicious food item.

Figuratively: There are things that everybody craves or seeks after. Who doesn't like a good thing?

Example: Awele went to the shop that had advertised free gifts for each customer arriving before 6 a.m. Given the early hour and the limited circulation of the advertisement, Awele was sure that the deal was privileged knowledge, and that there would be few people there. When he got there, guess what? There were throngs of people, some even fighting for their place in the line. And why not? After all, **Anụmanụ...**

Termite hill

Comment: Yes, every Enuani creature loves to eat the tasty flying termite. When the termites flock, animals that can be seen chasing after them include: toads, bats, chicken, flying birds, snakes, dogs, lizards, geckos, etc. Pretty much any animal with an appetite. Including humans. From all appearances, every animal is looking to eat the termite. Hence the saying.

✿ Anwụ gbáá nwata, ọ fụ-zị nzizi okpoloko ọ gba-a ọsọ

Literally: The child that has been stung by a bee takes flight on seeing a blowfly.

Figuratively: The source of an unpleasant experience tends to be avoided the next time around. Once bitten, twice shy.

Example: A friend once approached Awele and urged him to invest in a Ponzi scheme that would double his money in three months. Awele gullibly offered his money and in the end lost a lot. A couple  of years later, another friend who worked in a bank came to tell Awele about a new investment special that her bank was offering. This investment opportunity may have been genuine, but Awele could not be convinced. Once bitten, twice shy. **Anwụ...**

Comment: It is a natural human instinct to flee from anything that resembles what had previously posed a danger. Animals also share the same instinct, otherwise scarecrows would never be effective....This is similar to the Enuani proverb which states that having learned a lesson from an affliction, you should not go through the same affliction a second time: **Mbụ adị eme onye abụa eme ẹ.**

❀ Anya adị afụ nti

Literally: Your eyes can never see your ears.

Figuratively: Nature dictates that certain things just don't or can't happen.

Example: Awele narrated to his father in the village how a pastor in the city had been accused of sleeping with his own son's wife. To Awele's father and other village folk, this was an abomination. After marveling in horror at the abomination, Awele's father exclaimed that as far as conjugal relations between father and daughter-in-law were concerned, **Anya...**

Comment: This proverb apparently predates the advent of the mirror to Enuani. But it remains true if we are talking of your eyes seeing your ears directly. The proverb can be used in the context of anything that is forbidden or abnormal.

✿ Anya ka wa ji ama ọka cha-nị

Literally: You can tell a mature corn cob just by looking at it.

Figuratively: A good item or product manifests itself and is easy to discern.

Example: Of the five candidates for interview, one particularly stood out. She not only met the requirements, but she surpassed the others in experience, diction, and presentation. It was a no-brainer when the committee voted unanimously to offer her the job. **Anya ...**

Comment: A good product advertises itself.

✿ Aziza abụna ifé, mana chi foẹ ụtụtụ wa achọyalị a

Literally: The broom is of no consequence, but it is eagerly sought after at dawn each day.

Figuratively: Things that may seem inconsequential may often be indispensable because of the crucial roles they perform.

Example: When the junior workers union went on strike, Awele had to carry on his duties without his messenger. He was constrained to handle routine duties like fetching the mail, delivering packages, etc. The strike eventually ended, but not before Awele realized and appreciated the crucial role that the lowly messenger played in the running of his office. **Aziza...**

Comment: In nature, little things loom large. Take your eyes for example. They make up a very insignificant fraction of the weight of your body. And you take them for granted every day. But just think where you would be without them...There are basically two types of broom in traditional Enuani. One, made from palm fronds, is used mostly for sweeping the inside of the house. The other, made from the branches of the *Okakpa* shrub, is used mainly for sweeping the outside premises.

✿ Azụzụ na ụkwala bụ nwene

Literally: Catarrh and cough are siblings.

Figuratively: This is used for things or situations that are related or often occur together, whether positive or negative.

Example: Awele was not surprised to hear that the same fellow who was expelled from college for exam cheating had just been arrested for stealing from a supermarket. Cheating and theft are closely related. **Azụzụ...**

Comment: In most cases, catarrh and cough usually occur together, collaborating to make life miserable for a person with a cold or flu.... This is similar to the Enuani saying that the nose and the eye are related, such that when the nose has a cold, the eyes begin to weep: **Imi na anya bụ nwene; omẹẹ imi anya akwama.**

✿ Be onye bi ka ọ wachi

Literally: It is the place where you live that receives your roof-mending attention.

Figuratively: You look after yourself first, before looking out for others. Charity begins at home, before it spreads to other places.

Example: Awele had a sum of money that he wanted to donate to charity. Many far-flung charitable organizations were soliciting his donation. After deliberation, he decided to donate his money to the town union in his village which was trying to raise funds for a new health center. After all, **Be onye…**

Comment: The proverb, as written and said, specifically implies the mending of a thatched roof, the traditional roofing structure in Enuani. The leaf of the *Igbodo* plant was the preferred leaf of choice for constructing and mending of such roofs. These leaves fretted away quickly, and repairing the roof was a recurrent exercise. Naturally, you paid more attention to repairing your own roof, than to repairing any other person's roof.

✿ Be wa si adụụ nwa nwe nne ọdụ ka nwa enwenẹ nne si amalị ife

Literally: It is where the child with a mother is being advised that the child without a mother gets his own counsel.

Figuratively: You should try to learn from other people's mistakes, rather than waiting to learn from yours.

Example: Awele's colleague narrated to him how the police had given her a ticket for speeding on a particular stretch of road. Awele was due to travel that same road later that day, and she warned Awele to be careful. Sure enough, the police checkpoints were still there when Awele went through. But having been forewarned, he was on his best driving behavior. He had learned from his colleague's mistake. **Be wa...**

Comment: The smart person always tries to learn from the mistakes of others.

✿ Chukwu we imi nọchime ọnụ maka ife n'esii isi

Literally: God placed the nose close to the mouth to help prevent ingestion of putrefied smelly stuff.

Figuratively: This proverb is used in the context where the proximity of two items generates huge benefits or averts a disaster.

Example: Awele's aunt who lived in the same city suddenly had a heart attack. She was hospitalized for months on end. She had no children of her own, and depended entirely on Awele for financial and moral support. Everybody shuddered to think what would have happened to her if Awele was not nearby, willing and able to care for her. **Chukwu...**

Comment: The nose being close to the mouth is also beneficial in a positive sense. Fragrant and delicious food is often first sampled by the nose before the mouth gets a bite.

✺ Efi enwenẹ ọdụ̀ Chukwu ga achụ a nzizi

Literally: The cow without a tail relies on God to drive away the flies.

Figuratively: This proverb is used in the context where an underdog manages to survive or even thrive.

Example: Since Awele's aunt did not have a child of her own, how fortunate that she had Awele who treated her as a mother and provided all the care that she needed. **Efi enwenẹ...**

Comment: The poor, the sick, the oppressed, and all the underdogs of society; they all come under the category of the cow without a tail.

✿ Egbé beli, ugo beli; nke sị ibe ya ebenẹ nkwu akwalị a

Literally: The kite will perch, and the eagle will perch; may the curse of a broken wing come upon whichever prevents the other from perching.

Figuratively: Live and let live. Be tolerant of other people's needs and opinions.

Example: Awele is a Christian; his father in the village practices animist traditional religion. But each of them allows the other ample berth to practice their religion, without animosity or ill feeling. **Egbé beli...**

Comment: The spirit of tolerance is a highly valued virtue in Enuani.

✿ Egwù adị ekwe ogili esii n'ofe

Literally: Fear does not let the fermented castor seed paste smell in the soup.

Figuratively: Fear of retribution restrains you from doing certain things. Out of fear, you dare not do them.

Example: When the corruption tribunal asked for submissions about corrupt officials, Awele was of two minds. He knew his boss was very corrupt. He had indeed witnessed several incidents of corrupt transactions. He told his friends that he would expose his boss. But Awele feared the wrath of his boss if Awele should expose him. In the end, Awele felt intimidated and chose to keep quiet. When his friend asked him why he did not go through with the plan, Awele simply replied that **Egwù...**

Comment: Virtually all parts of the fresh castor plant are poisonous, including the seeds (also called beans). Indeed this plant is the source of ricin, one of the deadliest poisons known on earth. But Enuani people long evolved a way to consume the castor bean. The beans are boiled, crushed, and allowed to ferment, resulting in a smelly but non-poisonous paste called *Ogili isi* (the smelly ogili). It is a smell that matches certain fetid cheeses in western circles. *Ogili isi* is a delicious condiment much used for making soups in Enuani.

✿ Elo bẹẹ ntị wa ajụ mbekwu

Literally: If the edge of the forest mushroom has been nibbled, you should ask the tortoise.

Figuratively: Based on past patterns, certain infractions usually lead to the usual suspects.

Example: The cookie jar in Awele's household was the favorite haunt of Joe, his eldest son. All the other five children in the house liked cookies too, but were not as persistent  in raiding the cookie jar as Joe was. So, two days before Easter, their mother bought a special batch of cookies to be served to guests on Easter day. Come Easter morning, a significant portion of the special cookies had gone missing. Without bothering to involve the other children, Awele zeroed in on Joe for inquiries about the missing cookies. **Elo bẹẹ...**Awele's suspicions were confirmed when Joe confessed.

Comment: In Enuani folk lore and folk tales, the tortoise had pride of place for featuring more than any other animal. His cunning exploits formed the substance of many moonlight tales. Supposedly, one of his favorite snacks was nibbling on mushrooms in the lonely expanses of the dense tropical forest.

✿ Esu wa zọ ụkwụ akwana ákwá mana onye zọ a ya asị n'ụya egbuẹ yẹ

Literally: The millipede that's stepped upon is not fussing or screaming, but the person who did the stepping is cussing, shouting and lamenting his fate.

Figuratively: While the victim is silent, the victimizer is the one shouting and seeking to be pitied. This proverb is relevant in cases of gross injustice.

Example: As Awele was walking along the dirt road that was full of potholes, a taxi driver sped by, bumped into one of the potholes, and sent a splash of muddy water all over Awele's clothing. Rather than pity the pedestrian, the taxi driver popped out his head and cursed Awele for not giving way. As he sped away, the driver, for good measure, flung out his hand and offered an obscene gesture to Awele. It was clearly a case of, **Esu wa...**

Comment: In the era when Enuani people walked around mostly on bare feet, stepping on millipedes was a common occurrence. It was an unpleasant experience for the person walking. But nobody bothered to ask the millipede how he felt about the whole episode... This proverb is similar to the Enuani saying that the snail thrown to roast in the fire is not screaming, while the person who threw it complains that the snail's juices are extinguishing his fire: **Ilọma wa tinye n'ọkwụ´ akpọna mkpu, mana onye tinye ẹ ni asị n'ọgbọnyụsịa ọkwụ´.**

✿ Ewii tụa ọnụ, ọ tụa ụpụ

Literally: When the rabbit makes its burrow, it also makes an escape outlet.

Figuratively: As you go about executing plans, you should always have an alternative plan (a plan B) as a backup. Do not put all your eggs in one basket.

Example: Even though Awele's daughter had been admitted to one of the elite colleges, the family still pressed on with the admission applications for other colleges, just in case. **Ewii tụa...**

Comment: *Ewii* is variously rendered in English as the rabbit or the giant rat. It is a sizeable animal, with the bigger ones almost as large as a small cat. It is mainly nocturnal, spending most of the day in its burrow. Enuani people usually catch it in their traps, or dig the animal's burrows to find them. It is in this digging process that many Enuani kids learn that the *Ewii* always has a second outlet to the surface. Unless this second outlet is located and guarded, the quarried animal often escapes through it while the primary outlet is being exploited. Although crucial in *Ewii's* escape strategy, this second outlet probably serves an equally important biological function. It makes for air flow and cross ventilation through the entire burrow.

❀ Ewu a-ta ụza dị ndụ

Literally: The goat that is quietly chewing cod is alive.

Figuratively: A lull in activity is not a sign of extinction.

Example: Awele's good friend and frequent companion left for studies in the US. Overwhelmed by his new environment, he was negligent of his communication responsibilities. For  nearly three months after he left Awele, nothing was heard from him, and Awele was beginning to wonder whether he was alive or dead. Then, one day he telephoned Awele. He apologetically informed Awele that despite his lack of communication, he was still alive and well, though just barely ticking over. **Ewu a-ta...**

Comment: Many children in Enuani can't forget the picture of the goat lying contentedly under the eaves, doing nothing but chewing away for hours on end. Other ruminants, such as sheep and cattle, are also fond of this habit. Sometimes, the goat lies so still that you think it is dead. But as long as the mouth is moving, you are reassured that it is alive.

✿ Ewu ká ahụ ụsịa, ọ kaa ahụ ugbolo

Literally: The goat that's in the habit of stealing should equally be inured to being hit with a pole.

Figuratively: You should be ready for the consequences, however severe, of whatever you undertake.

Example: Awele's friend wanted to impress the community. Contrary to everybody's advice, he went and bought a very expensive latest-model car. The insurance bill alone was double what Awele was paying for his car. Then the maintenance bill came and it was triple what he was used to paying. He was furious, and complained bitterly to Awele. But Awele laughed at him, reminding him that what he was experiencing was what people with expensive cars go through. Since he was up to buying the big car, he had better be up to the maintenance expenses involved. **Ewu ká ahụ...**

Comment: In earlier times, free-roaming goats were a menace in Enuani village markets. The goats went briskly between market wares, taking bites from yams, cassava, or any other product on display. The market women, in turn, had wooden canes, poles or rods (*Ugbolo*) with which they hit the goats as they rampaged through. The more persistent goats apparently had become inured to the *Ugbolo*.

✿ Ezí afà ka ego

Literally: A good name is better than money.

Figuratively: It is more important to have a good name and high integrity, even at the risk of not being rich.

Example: Awele's father in the village advised him frequently to avoid the pervasive corruption in the city offices. Awele's boss was corrupt and had become rich in the process. But most people regarded him negatively and his name had been sullied. Awele, on the other hand, was not rich and was liable to the temptations of corruption. But his father constantly reminded him that a good name is better than riches. **Ezí afa...**

Comment: The preservation of a good name is an inter-generational goal in virtually all human societies.

✾ Gboo ka wa ji achubaa ewu ojii

Literally: The black goat should be corralled home and tethered before dusk.

Figuratively: Prevention is better than cure. It is better to take preventive action than to have to deal with the adverse consequences of delay. A stitch in time saves nine.

Example: Awele's father was having breathing difficulties with heart palpitations, and was receiving treatment from traditional village healers. He rejected Awele's moves to take him to the hospital in the city for examination. Instead he told Awele that he would only go to the hospital in four months' time, after the current farming season was over. But Awele continued pressing. He argued that since nobody knew the nature of the ailment, it was best to catch it early. **Gboo ka...**

Comment: The black goat was hard to see after dark. That was why it had to be rounded up early for the night. All Enuani goats were free-roaming in earlier times. While most goats found their night stalls on their own, a few had to be rounded up by the children and corralled for the night.

✸ Gidigidi na ádá wị

Literally: Too much hurry is accompanied by a fall.

Figuratively: Haste makes waste. Hurrying too much can lead to mistakes.

Example: In her hurry to catch her overseas flight, Awele's friend forgot her passport at home. Of course, she was denied travel on that day. Her inordinate haste had led to her error. **Gididi na...**

Comment: Good time management is a good antidote to *Gididi* (undue haste) and the consequent proneness to error.... This is similar to the Enuani saying about the hurry-hurry person that went to fetch water at the stream with a basket: **Omè k'ọkẹlẹ, ya ji nkata je iyi.**

✿ Ị maka àchà imi nkitẹ ọ ga na-ejilili nji

Literally: However much you wash the nose of a dog, that nose will still remain black.

Figuratively: Some things or characteristics are indelible. They have staying power, whatever you do.

Example: One of Awele's relatives was addicted to alcohol. He went through various rehabilitation programs, but always relapsed. He even tried patronizing a prayer house which claimed to treat such matters. But six months after the program, he was back to his alcoholic ways. **Ị maka…**

Comment: Most dog breeds in Enuani have black noses, even though world-wide, there are breeds with noses of other colors.... This saying is used mostly where an undesirable characteristic or trait persists despite strenuous efforts to eradicate it.

✿ Ibu ányị danda

Literally: A heavy load is never too much for the leafcutter ant.

Figuratively: This saying is relevant in situations where a person or thing seems capable of carrying surprisingly heavy loads or responsibilities.

Example: A big tree stood at the site where the new health center was to be built. Villagers wondered how in the world anybody could bring down that tree. Then one morning, the work crew came with a bulldozer. In only a few minutes of pushing and tugging, the bulldozer had felled the obstinate tree. Many of the onlookers were amazed at the brute strength of the bulldozer, all the time exclaiming, **"Ibu ányị..."**

Comment: The leafcutter ants are a common feature in Enuani forests and bushes, with their almost military-like formations trailing for long distances. People often marveled at how these ants could carry items that were many times their body weight.

✿ Ibu baá n'ụyà wa ebulu ẹ n'isi ọkpọlọ

Literally: If it comes to a matter of honor, you don't mind carrying the load on the bare head without the usual pad.

Figuratively: When it comes to upholding or defending honor, people are willing to endure extreme suffering and deprivation.

Example: Despite being relatively poor, Awele decided to enroll his daughter in an excellent but costly private school that his boss's children were attending. He considered it a matter of honor to provide the best education for his child. He was willing to make any sacrifice required to achieve the goal, including cancelling his vacation plans. **Ibu baá…**

Comment: In Enuani, the concept of *Ụyà* is a very delicate one that is difficult to translate into English. It somehow combines elements of honor, regret, remorse and pride. In any case, *Ụyà* is a significant dimension of feeling among Enuani people….In Enuani, heavy loads are normally carried on the head, not on the back or shoulders as in some other cultures. To soften the impact of the load on the head, the load rests on a pad usually made of curled-up cloth or leaves. Carrying the load on the bare head was unusual and punishing.

✿ Ifé nwe mbido, nwe ngwụsị

Literally: Whatever has a beginning has an ending.

Figuratively: Nothing lasts for ever. This too shall pass.

Example: During the time when Awele was jobless, he attended numerous interviews and received over a dozen rejection letters. During those dark days of despair, his mother always consoled him by reminding him that his desperate situation would end some day. **Ifé nwe...**

Comment: This saying is ideal as a consolation while enduring an adversity.

✿ Ikené madụ na nke ọ lụpụ, ume adị a lụa ọzọ

Literally: Thanking someone for what they have done gives them courage to do more.

Figuratively: Gratitude encourages more good works.

Example: Even though Awele's aunt could not repay Awele for his total care of her, she always expressed deep gratitude to Awele and praised him greatly to his face and to other relatives. This grateful posture was a morale booster for Awele and encouraged him to do more for her. **Ikené madụ...**

Comment: It's always good to be grateful.

✿ Ikwukwu kwuẹ wa afụ ikè ọkwụkwụ

Literally: It's when the wind blows that you can see the anus of the domestic fowl (chicken).

Figuratively: It's in situations of stress or adversity that you can tell who has mettle and who does not have it. A stress test will break the weak and manifest the strong.

Example: When Awele's aunt was in good health and relatively rich, all kinds of relatives and friends flocked around her. It was difficult to tell who was genuinely committed to her and who was not. When eventually she fell upon hard times and became sickly, most of those friends and relatives deserted her. Only Awele and one other relative remained faithful to her. The hard times had exposed the fake associates, leaving only those that were genuine. **Ikwukwu kwuẹ...**

Comment: Yes, the anus of the domestic fowl is usually concealed from view by tufts of feathers. But the occasional gust of wind lifts the feathers and exposes the anus.

🥀 Ilọma wa tinye n'ọkwụ́ akpọna mkpu, mana onye tinye ẹ ni asị n'ọgbọnyụsịa ọkwụ́

Literally: The snail that's thrown in the fire to roast is not screaming, but the person who threw it there is complaining that the juices expressed by the snail are extinguishing his fire.

Figuratively: This is used in cases of injustice, with the victimizer blaming the victim.

Example: The taxi driver splashed muddy water on Awele the pedestrian, then popped out his head to curse Awele for not giving way.

Comment: Snails, especially the big ones, are a major food delicacy in Enuani. Snails that are too small to be used in the main meal are usually given to the children, who in turn throw them in the fire to roast, before eating them. As the snail roasts, it exudes copious amounts of juices into the fire, threatening to extinguish the fire.... This saying is very similar to the one about the millipede that is stepped on. The millipede does not complain, while the barefoot stepper complains and bemoans his fate: **Esu wa zọ ụkwụ akwana ákwá mana onye zọ a ya asị n'ụya egbuẹ yẹ.**

✿ Imi na anya bụ nwene; o mẹẹ imi anya akwama

Literally: The nose and the eye are relatives; when the nose is ailing, the eyes start to weep tears.

Figuratively: This saying is used to highlight the interconnectedness of things or people.

Example: When the company disciplined one employee for flimsy reasons, all the other employees went on strike in sympathy. Even though the current disciplinary action did not affect them directly, they wanted to rally on their colleague's behalf. **Imi na...**

Comment: It's indeed true that when you have a cold or runny nose, the eyes usually chime in sympathetically to produce tears... This is similar to the Enuani saying that catarrh and cough are related: **Azụzụ na ụkwala bụ nwene.**

❀ Isí anyụna ahụlụ mana o bulu ọkpọ

Literally: The head did not utter the offending fart, but *it* receives the punitive knock.

Figuratively: This is used in cases where the wrong person is punished for the crime, and there has been a miscarriage of justice.

Example: The messenger was handed a summons to deliver to the accused at their home. When he got to their home, he was subjected to verbal and physical abuse. In vain he tried to explain that he was only given the item to deliver, and had no say in the legal process. It was a classic case of **Isí anyụna...**

Comment: Among groups of village Enuani children, farting was considered offensive, and was sometimes punished with a knock on the head delivered by the older kids. Maybe a spanking on the buttocks might have brought the punishment closer to the offending organ...This proverb is similar to the one saying that conveying the message should not pose harm to the messenger: **Ozi adị egbu ụkọ.**

✿ Isi iyi ka mmili na-esi agbalụ-ha

Literally: The muddying of the stream water usually starts from the headwaters.

Figuratively: The dominant person or thing usually sets the example that others follow.

Example: When Awele's colleagues noticed that their boss was corrupt, they saw it as a license for them to engage in corrupt practices as well. Had the boss not been corrupt, they themselves would not have become corrupt in turn. **Isi iyi...**

Comment: This saying is usually used for situations where the leader sets a bad example which everybody else then follows.

❀ Ji adị esi ọdụ` epu

Literally: Yam does not sprout from its tail end.
Figuratively: Things have a certain order of precedence.
Example: At the Enuani village gathering, the novice server

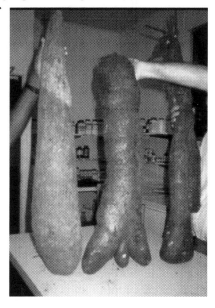

was presenting the cup of palm wine to the young but rich businessman who came down from the city. This happened even though some of the elders had not yet been served, and ignoring the usual age order for serving palm wine. One of the elders called the server to order, reminding him that **Ji adị...**

Comment: Yam, culturally the most important food product in Enuani tradition, always sprouts from the head end. Only if you cut it into several pieces will the non-head pieces attempt to sprout. But even then, they will sprout from the end that was originally closest to the head. Since the yam tuber is the primary means of propagating the crop, the sprouting of the tuber is agriculturally very significant.... This proverb is slightly similar to the Enuani proverb that asserting your rights should not be considered greedy: **Mụ k'olu abụna ụsịa.** It is also similar to the saying that you cannot snap your fingers without the thumb: **Wa adị ahapụ isi aka agba ụlịọ.**

197

❀ Ka agwụụ agwụna ị lu, ị ma sị ka ịfịa ọnwụ we ile i no

Literally: However desperately hungry you are, you don't begin to feed on your tongue.

Figuratively: Despite dire straits, there's a limit to how much compromise you can make.

Example: Despite his relative poverty and the pervasive corruption in his workplace, Awele resolved to suffer rather than yield to the temptation of corruption. **Ka agwụụ...**

Comment: Yes, your tongue is readily available, and a meaty chunk at that. But you don't contemplate consuming it even if you're dying of hunger. A related aphorism is that if you consume your tongue when you are hungry, what will you do when food comes and you need to taste it? It's like a farmer who's so hungry that he consumes all the seeds that were intended for planting. How will he generate the next crop? [*This is an original saying from Inno Onwueme]...* This proverb is similar to the one about the greedy caterpillar that eats up the leaf that provides it shade: **Ọbụbụ nwekẹ anya úkwú ọ tachapụụ akwụkwọ kpudo ẹ ndo.** It is also similar to the one that says that however much the native soap deteriorates, it is never infested by maggots: **Ncha lekẹ ule ọ dị esu ọkọlị.**

✿ Ka ị chụ odudu, ka ọ táá onye?

Literally: When you swat away the tsetse fly, whom do you expect it to bite?

Figuratively: This saying applies in instances where one person is shirking his responsibility and leaving it to others to discharge.

Example: Awele's village did not have electricity. Rather than using their clout to agitate for electrification, the few prominent people from the village had each procured an electricity generator for their households. Each person considered it someone else's responsibility to mobilize for action to electrify the entire village. When Awele spoke at the annual village gathering, he deplored the situation. He ended by querying the gathered dignitaries, **"Ka ị chụ…"**

Comment: Yes, the tsetse fly, which causes sleeping sickness, has been historically present in Enuani, though not in large numbers. Its presence has been blamed for the inability to carry on extensive cattle husbandry in Enuani.

❀ Ma chi ejinẹ, wa adị akalụ ụbọsị

Literally: If the day is not over, you should not declare that day as unproductive.

Figuratively: Withhold judgement until all the evidence and data are in. Do not rush to judgement.

Example: Awele's friend entered the building materials business during a slump in the economy. Many well-wishers advised him against it, but he persisted. A few months later, the economy rebounded; his business picked up and now those who judged him prematurely have come to appreciate his strategy. **Ma chi...**

Comment: The rush to judgement often can lead to erroneous judgement.

❀ Ma ọnwụ egbunẹ nwa ọkẹtẹ o mẹẹ tẹ nne nkwụ

Literally: If death spares the young palm tree sapling, it will grow to be a huge mother tree.

Figuratively: From striving wretched beginnings, you could pull through to thriving prosperous existence.

Example: Awele's cousin had a hard time making it through school. He failed and had to repeat practically every grade. Then he struggled through college with only mediocre grades. Everybody had given up hope on him making anything useful out of himself. But look at him now. He has blossomed into a successful businessman, with substantial standing in the community. Given how he started, nobody would ever have thought it. **Ma ọnwụ...**

Comment: The African Oil Palm tree is the most significant indigenous tree in Enuani. The tree plays a role in every facet of Enuani life. Its provisions include palm oil for cooking, thatch for roofing, palm wine for socio-cultural purposes, timber for building, brooms for sweeping, etc. Indeed, Enuani culture has evolved to utilize virtually all parts of the tree.

✿ Ma onye alachana mgbemgbe ọnụ a, ụgwụlụ analị a ya

Literally: If you don't lick your lips to moisten them, the dry harmattan wind will snatch them from you.

Figuratively: If you don't take care of your own, nobody else will, and it will go to waste.

Example: Awele's friend was very negligent in his parental duties towards his only son. All the moral and emotional supports of a father were denied to the child. As he grew into adolescence, the boy sought such support and mentorship from others. Soon he was taken in by a cult of older friends that provided support for him, but indulged in all kinds of crimes. It was only too late that the father realized his mistake, and all attempts to reestablish a relationship with the boy failed. Since the father failed to do his duty in the early years, more sinister characters had stepped into the breach. **Ma onye...**

Comment: The dry harmattan wind blows from the Sahara desert through Enuani around December/January. It is indeed a phenomenon to watch out for. Apart from the ubiquitous dust that it brings, it wreaks havoc on the skin and lips. It's best to keep them moist to minimize the harm. This dry wind also fans many forest fires that break out in Enuani during the dry season.

✿ Madụ bụ chi ibe ẹ

Literally: Each person is a guardian angel to the other.

Figuratively: We are dependent on one another. We are our brother's (and sister's) keepers.

Example: Without Awele's input, where would his indigent and sickly aunt be today? Awele is almost like her *Chi*. **Madụ bụ...**

Comment: The concept of "*Chi*" in Enuani cosmology is something like a personal god, roughly equivalent to the western concept of a guardian angel. Each person has a unique *Chi* of his own. The *Chi* navigates him through his destiny and performs a general protective role.

✿ Mbụ adị eme onye abụa eme ẹ

Literally: Having learned a lesson from an affliction, you should not go through the same affliction a second time.

Figuratively: Fool me once, shame on you; fool me twice, shame on me.

Example: On their first visit back to their remote village after many years, Awele and his family were pretty careless in terms of their health issues. After all, this was their home village, so what harm could come to them? They ate and drank at will, and walked around in scanty clothing without protection from insect bites. Everything went well, but the consequences came within a few days of their return to their domicile in the city. They all had diarrhea from eating food of questionable provenance. Worse still, the two younger children each went through a severe bout of malaria, the result of mosquito bites in the village. So, the next time Awele and his family visited the village, everybody was on guard to prevent a repeat of the earlier pattern. **Mbụ adị...**

Comment: Once bitten twice shy....This is similar to the Enuani proverb which says that the child that has been stung by a bee takes flight on seeing a blowfly: **Anwụ gbáá nwata, ọ fụ-zị nzizi okpoloko ọ gba-a ọsọ.**

❀ Me m megwalị adị esee okwu

Literally: If you do me wrong, my retaliation should not cause a dispute.

Figuratively: Revenge or retaliation is only fair.

Example: For many months, Awele's antagonistic workmate had been maligning him and rubbishing his image with the boss. His antics included many falsehoods that he told to the boss. But the workmate was not clean either; he had many skeletons of his own in his cupboard. After tolerating his antics for a while, Awele decided to retaliate by letting the boss know some of the workmate's dirty secrets. Awele justified his action by saying to himself, **"Me m megwalị..."**

Comment: This saying is often rendered in local pidgin English as, "Do me, I do you, God no go vex"....This proverb is similar to the Enuani proverb which says that if someone uses trickery to hurt you, you use trickery to retaliate: **Nwata gbe igbe anị hụ ị ọkwụ igbe igbe anị hụgwalị a.**

❀ Mgba aja da-nị ha nwa ewu ji nwe iké lịkwasị a

Literally: It's only because the wall has fallen that the little goat is able to climb on top of it.

Figuratively: When the high brings itself low, don't be surprised if it becomes the subject of insults. Respect has to be earned. Persons behaving in a disrespectful manner should not expect to be respected.

Example: Awele's uncle was a womanizer. Despite his advanced age, he continued to run after young girls. In the process, he often clashed with the competing young boys, and lost all respect among village youth. The loss of respect was dramatized one day when one of the boys slapped him at the village meeting. This was a huge public disgrace, but could not have come if he had not lowered himself to the level of those boys. **Mgba aja...**

Comment: The wall implied in this proverb is the mud wall that was common in traditional Enuani society. Depending on the strength of the mud, sections of the wall could crack and ultimately come tumbling down. This gave the free-roaming goats the opportunity to clamber on top of the wall that was previously beyond their reach.

✽ Mgbamgba kross abụna mgbamgba okwukwe

Literally: A huge cross is not a sign of huge faith.

Figuratively: Appearances can be deceiving. Watch out for showy or pretentious individuals who have very little substance to them.

Example: When the launching ceremony was done for the new health center, one bombastic businessman came forward and pledged to donate a huge sum of money. It was by far the largest pledge of the day. Everybody cheered him on with accolades and praises from all directions. One year after the launching, the businessman had not redeemed his pledge. Right up till when construction of the health center was finished, the businessman still had not redeemed his pledge. Having basked in the publicity of his pledge, it was now clear that there was no substance to his pomposity. **Mgbamgba kross...**

Comment: This must be a latter-day saying, since it must have arisen after Christianity came to Enuani. It applies almost literally to the flourishing evangelist industry that has gripped Enuani in the first decades of the 21st century. Loud crosses on bogus buildings are accompanied by equally bogus proclamations and claims. Showy outward manifestations are no measure of inward authenticity or piety.

❀ Mili madụ ga alá ama hufe ẹ

Literally: The water destined to be drunk by you will not flow past you.

Figuratively: What is destined to happen must happen.

Example: During the hopeless days when Awele was jobless, he received one rejection letter after another. As he began to despair, his friend consoled him by telling him that these missed jobs were not destined for him. Somewhere out there, there was a job specifically destined for him. And that was precisely what happened a few months later. **Mili madụ...**

Comment: Belief in destiny is strong in Enuani. This is also related to the concept of C*hi* or personal god which guides each person's destiny.

✿ Mkpịsịaka nine ahana

Literally: Fingers are not all equal.

Figuratively: Some things, persons, or situations are better endowed than others.

Example: When Awele applied to his company for sponsorship to undertake a management course, he was denied. His boss who applied at the same time was successful, mainly because of his seniority. They both were employees, but some were more highly placed than others. All employees were not equal. **Mkpịsịaka...**

Comment: More often, this saying is used to imply differences in destiny between various persons. All destinies are not equal....This proverb is similar to the one about the lizard and the rat getting wet, with the lizard drying out quickly while the rat remains wet: **Oke na ngwele daa mmili, ọ-kọa ngwele ọma kọ oke.**

✿ Mkpụlụ ogili gbụẹ onye, ífé ọma gbu ẹ

Literally: If the melon *Ogili* seed kills you, you've been killed by a good thing.

Figuratively: It is worth it to suffer adversity for a good cause.

Example: When Awele's cousin fell off the canoe accidentally, his father jumped into the river to try to save him, even though the father could not swim. The father didn't care if he himself drowned in the process. **Mkpụlụ...**

Comment: In Enuani, the edible melon seed is called *Ogili* or *Egusi*. It is unclear why *Ogili* was chosen as the subject of this proverb.

✹ Mmụta abụna ngala

Literally: Knowledge acquired through learning is not arrogance.

Figuratively: By exercising your knowledge, you are not necessarily showing off.

Example: Awele's car suddenly started running poorly and belching smoke. He spent many weekends trying to fix the problem himself, including many hours crawling under the car. When he finally reached the limit of his knowledge, he called in his mechanic cousin to help out. Within five minutes, the mechanic had identified the problem, made minor adjustments to the engine, and got it running smoothly again. As he proudly accepted congratulations and thanks from Awele for his mechanical knowledge, he jokingly reminded Awele that **Mmụta...**

Comment: This saying reminds us that knowledge is most appreciated when it is exercised with humility and consideration. We should never take advantage of our superior knowledge to lord it over others.

✿ Mụ ka olu abụna ụsịa

Literally: Asserting that it is my turn does not indicate greedy appetite.

Figuratively: Asserting my right should not be misconstrued as being too forward or acquisitive.

Example: Awele was passed over for study leave even though it was his turn. He complained bitterly to his auntie and sought her advice. She consoled him, but insisted that Awele's rights had been violated. She advised Awele to write a protest petition to the higher authorities. To dispel Awele's hesitancy to write the petition, she reminded him that nobody could accuse him of being too greedy simply for asserting his rights. **Mụ ka olu...**

Comment: This proverb is set in the context of the village gathering where some communal livestock had been slaughtered and was being shared. After the meat has been divided up into portions and displayed, individuals took their pick in strict order of age seniority. It was a serious infraction to pick when it was not your turn. Conversely, you were expected to assert your right to pick as soon as everybody older than you had taken their pick.... This proverb is similar to the Enuani proverb that yam does not sprout from the tail: **Ji adị esi ọdụ̀ epu.** Things have a certain order of precedence.

✿ Ncha lekẹ ule ọ dị esu ọkọlị

Literally: However much the native soap deteriorates and softens, you won't see maggots in it.

Figuratively: Whatever the adversity, there are limits to how much compromise you should be willing to make.

Example: Awele's uncle had fallen on hard times. Despite his physical and financial weakness, he insisted that he must continue to pay the school fees required to keep his son in school. He downsized most aspects of his life, but the one area he was not willing to compromise was the upbringing of his children. He might be down and out in most aspects of his life, but it did not extend to this one aspect. He asserted that: **Ncha lekẹ...**

Comment: The traditional Enuani soap is usually made from palm oil (or palm kernel oil) using ashes derived by burning the husks from palm fruit bunches. The soap made from palm kernel oil is black and is used mainly for medicinal purposes. The more common soap is made from palm oil, and comes out as a greyish-brown crumbly mass. As it spends days in the soap container, it softens, which to the Enuani observer is equivalent to rotting. But this process is devoid of the maggots usually associated with rotting materials. Hence the saying....This proverb is somewhat similar to the one about not swallowing your tongue no matter how hungry you may get: **Ka agwụụ agwụna ị lu, ị ma sị ka ịfịa ọnwụ we ile i no.**

✿ Ngwele si enu daa, ma wa ajana a ọ sị ka ya jaa onwe yẹ

Literally: When the lizard jumps from a height, it looks around for praise. But finding none, it decides to praise itself (by nodding its head up and down).

Figuratively: Don't be surprised if nobody praises you for good deeds. Be content in yourself for having done the good deed.

Example: When Awele's cousin passed a very difficult professional exam, very few people in the village took notice. The few that knew about it did not appreciate what it was all about. But in  celebration, the cousin organized a grand party for herself in the city. Justifying her action to Awele, she explained that she was obliged to celebrate for herself, since nobody else was forthcoming to do it. **Ngwele si...**

Comment: The kind of lizard common in Enuani had the habit of dropping from great heights for no apparent reason. It would then commence the bobbing of the head which Enuani lore interpreted as self-congratulation... This proverb is similar to the Enuani proverb that the rejected/ostracized person does not reject himself: **Onye wa jụ adị ajụ onwe ẹ.**

214

✿ Nnà dị n'azụ bụ azụ

Literally: The dark caterpillar-like pest that infests dried fish is part of the fish.

Figuratively: You have to take the good with the bad that accompanies it. It's a package deal.

Example: Since childhood, Awele has loved eating beans, his favorite food item. In recent months, though, he discovered that he had indigestion and stomach discomfort each time he ate beans. The doctor told him that it was not a serious medical issue, and that beans are high in protein. So, Awele was torn between discontinuing his favorite food and tolerating the stomach discomfort. Eventually, he decided to continue eating beans, while tolerating the slight discomfort. **Nnà dị n'azụ bụ azụ.**

Comment: Dried fish in storage in Enuani was usually infested with *Nnà*, a small hairy dark worm resembling a caterpillar. Quite frequently, the *Nnà* showed up in the dishes that had been prepared using dried fish. But this was a normal expectation and caused little revulsion. Hence the saying.

✸ Nni bọa ọlà o mẹ-ẹ nke otu

Literally: Fufu that is left over till the next day becomes group property.

Figuratively: If the primary person responsible for something fails to discharge the responsibility, the community sometimes has to step in to take on the responsibility. Similarly, property that is neglected by the owner devolves to become communal property.

Example: The only son of one of the village elders was negligent in the care of his father. The son was away in the city and never visited his father, despite the old man's failing health. Noting the neglect, neighbors pitched in to run errands for the old man and even to help out in his farm work. Eventually, the community got together to raise money to send him to hospital for treatment. Since the son had failed in his duties, the community had to step in. **Nni bọa...**

Comment: In traditional Enuani society, yam fufu was the usual evening meal, eaten by separate groups in the household. Leftover fufu portions from the various groups were aggregated and formed all or part of the household breakfast the next morning. The morning meal, made up of the previous night's leftover fufu, was called *Nni ọlà*.

✿ Nni lẹlẹ azụ luẹ n'ime ọnụ ọ hapụ a aka ka wa gweli ẹ

Literally: The fufu cajoles the bit of fish into the mouth, then abandons it to be ground up through chewing.

Figuratively: Beware of people or situations that entice you into deep trouble and then abandon you to suffer the trouble unaided.

Example: Awele's teenage cousin had poor parents, but he was fond of hanging out with the children of the rich and famous. Those children taught him all kinds of mischief and petty crime which they committed all over town. When Awele sat his cousin down to advise him, Awele reminded him of the status of his companion mischief-makers. If they all got caught by police, the rich parents would find a way to free their children, while Awele's cousin would be left to bear the full brunt of the law. His companions would offer him no help, and would probably deny associating with him.

Comment: This proverb is keyed on the dynamics of eating fufu. When the fufu picks up a piece of fish (or meat) from the soup, the fufu is loaded into the mouth with the fish perched on it. Once in the mouth, the fufu is swallowed whole without being chewed, but the fish is not so lucky. It is subjected to intense mastication before it is eventually swallowed. *[* This is an original metaphor proverb by Inno Onwueme]*...This proverb is similar to the Enuani proverb about the lizard and the rat getting wet together. The lizard is able to dry out quickly, while the rat remains wet: **Oke na ngwele daa mmili, ọ-kọa ngwele ọma kọ oke.**

✿ Ntị anụ ókwú wa e-bee gwalị isi

Literally: The ear that fails to heed warnings winds up being cut off along with the head.

Figuratively: If the ear fails to heed warnings, the entire head may be at risk. Failure to heed warnings can have dire consequences.

Example: One of the young men in Awele's village was frequently caught stealing. The elders advised him on many occasions against this habit, but he persisted. Eventually, he moved to the city and to a higher level of thievery. Eventually, he was caught and sentenced to prison. When Awele heard the full story, he agreed with others that all this would have not happened had the man heeded the earlier advice. It was certainly a case of: **Ntị anụ ókwú wa e-bee gwalị isi.**

Comment: The moral of the proverb is simple: failure to heed advice can lead to grave misfortune.

✿ Nwa wa kwọ n'azụ amana n'ije dị ụfụ

Literally: The baby that is being carried on the back does not realize that the journey is tedious.

Figuratively: A person that is being supported often does not realize how difficult it is for the person generating the support.

Example: Awele's cousin was a spendthrift. Despite the poverty of his parents, he constantly demanded pocket money from them. He would then turn around to spend the money on fancy clothes, jewelry and other frivolities. He did not appreciate how much sacrifice and self-deprivation his parents were undertaking to come up with the money that they gave him. He was a free loader on a metaphoric gravy train. **Nwa wa kwọ n'azụ amana n'ije dị ụfụ.**

Comment: In traditional Enuani, there were no strollers for carrying babies while working or walking from place to place. Instead babies were carried on the mother's back, secured there by one or two pieces of cloth. This freed up the mother's hands for walking or discharging various tasks. Such babies, of course, had no appreciation of the mother's struggles with the weight of the baby and the task being discharged.

❀ Nwata gbe igbe anị hụ ị ọkwụ igbe igbe anị hụgwalị a

Literally: If a child crawls up and burns you with fire, you crawl up and exact revenge.

Figuratively: If someone deliberately hurts you through trickery, you hurt him back through trickery.

Example: Just as Awele's workmate was sneaking around with the boss trying to get Awele fired, Awele too was sneaking around spreading rumors about the workmate and damaging his credibility.

Comment: This proverb is somewhat similar to the Enuani proverb which says that exacting revenge is only fair and should not be cause for dispute: **Me m megwalị adị esee okwu.** It is also similar to the Enuani saying that when two clever experts do a transaction, neither party can have an undue advantage: **Amalịká na amàlịkà zụa afịa, elele adị adịa.**

✿ Nwata kwọa aka o soo ndị ka anya belịẹ nni

Literally: If a child washes his hands, he can dine on fufu with the adults.

Figuratively: If a young person shows enough maturity, he can be included in adult deliberations or activities.

Example: One precocious teenager in Awele's village was so smart that he finished his bachelor's degree by age 20. Along the way, he had traveled extensively on scholarship and was wise in the ways of the world. Despite his youthfulness, he was frequently invited to meetings of the village elders who then sought his opinion on various matters. His maturity had earned him a respected place among the elders. **Nwata...**

Comment: This proverb is based on the fact that fufu is usually eaten with bare hands, not with forks and spoons. It is necessary to wash the hands before dining on the fufu.

✤ Nwayọ nwayọ ka wa ji alacha ofe dị ọkwụ´

Literally: Soup that is hot will need to be consumed very cautiously.

Figuratively: Hectic or delicate situations must be handled with care and caution.

Example: Awele was nearly driven crazy by the many false accusations heaped upon him by his workmate who wanted to get him fired. He considered all kinds of damaging counter-measures. But his best friend advised him to take it easy, saying, **"Nwayọ…"**

Comment: In Enuani, soup is not something you sip with a spoon. Instead, it is a sauce into which you dip your ball of fufu before putting the fufu into your mouth and swallowing it without chewing. Whether it is the Enuani soup (such as *agbọnọ, egusi, nsala,* etc.) which is eaten with fingers with the fufu, or the foreign soup that you sip with a spoon, caution is equally applicable when the soup is piping hot.

✿ Nzizi sịa-ka ụsịa o soo nsị naa mmọ

Literally: The housefly with a huge appetite will follow the excrement and meet its doom.

Figuratively: An excessive appetite or craving can sometimes lead to disastrous consequences.

Example: A young man in the village had a huge craving for female companionship. His romantic exploits were well known and he had many girlfriends at a time. He even had a couple of children out of wedlock. All this complicated his life significantly, and he was unable to complete his education or to hold down a decent job. His passion for womanizing had led him to a miserable life. **Nzizi...**

Comment: With relatively shallow pit latrines as the norm in traditional Enuani, houseflies were a common sight around excrement.

✿ Ọbịa be onye abịágbúnẹ ẹ

Literally: May the visitor not take over your abode.

Figuratively: May the visitor not disrupt your life by causing you to lose control of your home or property. May the recipient not take undue advantage of your kindness.

Example: Due to a fire that ravaged his home, one villager sought refuge at Awele's village house. He was single and moved into one of the bedrooms in the house. A few weeks after moving in, he invited his brother to join him. Shortly after that, a friend of his also moved in. Eventually, their property spilled over into the living room. The kitchen and bathrooms were now dingy and busier than usual. When Awele visited, he was appalled by the deterioration of his house. His kindness had led to a virtual takeover of his house by the stranger. This should not be so. **Ọbịa...**

Comment: This proverb is similar to the Enuani proverb which says that when the owner of something is cheated by being assigned a minority share, the entire village will hear about it: **Wa linashị onye nweni idumu anụ.** It is also similar to the saying that it is the dog that you cuddle that winds up chewing on your clothing: **Wa patinye nwa nkite n'ahụ ọ takama ákwà.**

✿ Ọbụbụ nwekẹ anya úkwú ọ tachapụụ akwụkwọ kpudo ẹ ndo

Literally: The greedy caterpillar eats up the leaf that is providing it shade.

Figuratively: Greed can backfire on the greedy person and bring unpleasant consequences.

Example: The greedy businessman used his influence to acquire much property and land, some of it aggressively taken from others. Most people in the village  detested him for his greed. The crunch came when the businessman was suddenly arrested. Rather than rally to his cause as was usual for the villagers, everybody left him to stew in his own juice. His greed had dissipated the usual material support and social protection that the village normally provided to those in trouble. **Ọbụbụ…**

Comment: *[*This is an original proverb by Inno Onwueme]…* This proverb is similar to the one which says that however hungry you may be, you don't get desperate enough to swallow your tongue: **Ka agwụụ agwụna ị lu, ị ma sị ka ịfịa ọnwụ we ile i no.** It is also similar to the one about the person trying to lick the back of the ladle and spilling the contents of the ladle in the process: **Onye chọka nke dị azụ oziozi, nke dị ime ẹ ehufuẹ.**

✿ Odudu be-do n'akpa amụ akọ ka wa ji egbu ẹ

Literally: The tsetse fly that perches on the scrotum has to be killed with great caution.

Figuratively: Tricky or delicate situations require delicate handling.

Example: When Awele noticed that his father was having affairs with several women around town, he was not sure how to broach the delicate topic with his father. As a junior, he was not supposed to be prying into his father's romantic affairs. Yet, the situation was a threat to the family name and reputation. Eventually, Awele spoke to his father about it with all the delicacy and diplomacy he could muster. **Odudu...**

Comment: This proverb is fairly common in Enuani, but the situation it describes is a bit peculiar. It may have originated when Enuani people went about with no or scanty clothing; at least scanty enough to permit the tsetse fly access to the scrotum. From there, caution was needed to avoid doing more damage than the tsetse fly could have done....This is similar to the proverb that advises caution when eating hot soup: **Nwayọ nwayọ ka wa ji alacha ofe dị ọkwụ́.**

✸ Ofigbo tụ-ka ji nwata ọ nama okei anya

Literally: If the child's yam is too much suffused with palm oil, it becomes enticing to the adult.

Figuratively: Things that you would normally ignore may become attractive if sufficiently adorned or decorated.

Example: Awele took his child to the playground. He was impressed by how much his child and other adolescent children were enjoying the swing. On a whim, he climbed onto the swing and allowed himself to ride for a few minutes. When his friend teased him about it, he defended himself by saying that he was enticed by how much fun the kids were having on the swing. **Ofigbo...**

Comment: Palm oil is the traditional edible oil in Enuani. It is called *ofigbo* or *mmanụ*. Its bright red color makes it an attractive condiment not only for cooking, but in this case, to accompany boiled or roasted yam.

✿ Oge onye ji bunii bụ ụtụtụ a

Literally: The time of your departure is your morning.

Figuratively: The time when you commence a journey or activity is your prime time, irrespective of when other people commenced.

Example: Awele's auntie did not go to school as a child. She was already in middle age when she started attending adult education classes. Some villagers teased her that she was competing with children for school books. But Awele encouraged her by telling her the many advantages of being literate, and reminding her that this time was as good as any for her to start schooling. **Oge onye...**

Comment: Farming was the most common profession in traditional Enuani. With the sun's intensity under the ambient tropical conditions, it was prudent to rise early and do most of the day's work in the morning, before the heat set in. So, the morning was marked as the best time to get anything done.

✿ ´Ọgọ` bụ chi onye

Literally: Your relatives-in-law are like your guardian angels.

Figuratively: You expect a lot of mutual dependency and friendly interaction between you and your relatives-in-law.

Example: When Awele's father-in-law was being installed as a chief in the village, most of his blood relatives were lukewarm since they believed that somebody else among them deserved the chieftaincy. But Awele and his own relatives did their best to make up the deficit. They came through in a big way with financial, moral and social support. ´Ọgọ` bụ ...

Comment: In Enuani society, it is expected that the relationship between in-laws should be cherished and nurtured. This is done by frequent exchanges of gifts and favors. In traditional Enuani, the wife's relatives were particularly expected to receive gifts and favors from the man and his relatives. Some of these gifts and favors were formal and expected. Others were casual and occasional, including helping out when there was trouble or a death in the family of the in-laws. *Ọgọ bụ chi onye* is a mantra that is heard frequently when the kolanut is being broken during visits by the in-laws.

❀ Ogoli ṇua di nabị ọ ma-lị nke ka mma

Literally: When a woman has had two husbands, she is able to discern which one was better.

Figuratively: When you've experienced two different situations or things, then you can tell which one was better. The grass is not always greener on the other side. Look before you leap.

Example: Awele's cousin came from the village to look for work in the city. He stayed with Awele, but was chafing that Awele was too strict and did not allow him to go out at night. In protest, he moved over to the house of another of their relatives. Less than a month later, Awele heard that the relative had kicked him out for staying out late at night. Soon, he was back, begging Awele to accommodate him. Having tasted the two situations, he was now the wiser as to which was better. **Ogoli ṇua...**

Comment: This proverb is used most often in a situation of regret where a person has abandoned one thing or situation for another that is not necessarily better....The usual Enuani word for Woman is *Okpoho*. Peculiarly, it is in proverbs and metaphors that one encounters *Ogoli* as a word for Woman.

❧ Ojeko egbu m gbuẹ onwẹ ẹ

Literally: The person trying to kill me winds up killing himself in the process.

Figuratively: May the ill will of my enemy backfire and turn on the enemy himself.

Example: While laying administrative traps for Awele to get him fired, his coworker told many lies. Eventually, the manager discovered his lies and issued him a letter of warning. In his effort to harm Awele, the coworker had wound up harming himself.

Comment: This proverb can be rendered as a statement, or as a prayerful wish…. It is similar to the one which says that the master trickster winds up tricking himself: **Ọkantụ tụka ọ tụa onwẹ ẹ.**

✿ Ọjị́ luẹ ụnọ o kwuẹ onye che ẹ ni

Literally: When the kolanut gets home, it will say who initially offered it to guests.

Figuratively: A piece of kolanut, taken home after visiting, is a reminder and indication of the person that was visited.

Example: Awele's father paid a visit to the chief. After the kolanut ceremonies, the father pocketed the leftover kolanut, vowing to share it with his wife when he got home, to let her know that he had been to the chief's house. **Ọjị́ luẹ...**

Comment: Kolanut is the culturally symbolic item that is presented to guests as a sign of welcome by the Enuani person. The kolanut is ceremonially broken by the oldest person, who recites incantations and traditional prayers in the process. After that, the kolanut pieces are passed around for those present to pick in descending order of age. Any leftover pieces of kolanut are given to the guests as a symbol of their visit, and as a reminder of the occasion after they've returned home....The cultural significance of the kolanut pervades all of Enuani life. It is the item that must be present in culturally important gift-giving, fine-paying, and communal gatherings. When feasible, the kolanut is accompanied by palm wine, the traditional cultural beverage in Enuani.

✿ Ọkantụ tụka ọ tụa onwẹ ẹ

Literally: The master trickster winds up tricking himself.

Figuratively: Deviousness and trickery, when carried to extremes, will eventually backfire on the trickster.

Example: The fake pastor was in the habit of collecting money from students, with the promise that he would use his spiritual powers to get them through exams. Unfortunately, this promise lulled most of the students into laziness, and many of them failed the exam. The pattern was repeated several times. Eventually, his student clientele dropped drastically, and even his ordinary parishioners deserted him as a fake. His ministry collapsed and his worship house was destroyed. **Ọkantụ...**

Comment: This proverb is similar to the one about the person trying to harm me winding up harming himself: **Ojeko egbu m gbuẹ onwẹ ẹ.**

✿ Oké na ngwele daa mmili, ọ-kọa ngwele ọma kọ oké

Literally: When the lizard and the rat jump into water together, the lizard is able to dry out quickly, while the rat remains wet.

Figuratively: Each person's destiny or fate is unique and different. People that you join in bad deeds may have a way of escaping punishment, while you get punished. Watch out for bad company.

Example: One of Awele's workmates joined some rich people in investing in a pyramid scheme that promised to double their money in a short time. Unfortunately, the scheme collapsed and the investors lost their money. While the rich people could well afford their lost investment, the workmate could not. She was reduced to poverty. She had made the mistake of joining people who were above her economic level. In the end, she was the only one that was devastated. **Oké na…**

Comment: This proverb is similar to the one about all fingers not being of the same length: **Mkpịsịaka nine ahana….** It is also similar to the one about fufu leading the fish condiment into the mouth and letting go for the fish to be crushed: **Nni lẹlẹ azụ luẹ n'ime ọnụ ọ hapụ a aka ka wa gweli ẹ.**

✿ Okei bụ ụnọ

Literally: The male child is the home.

Figuratively: The male child is a key pillar of the home.

Example: When Awele's grandfather died, his father inherited all the family property, even though Awele's father had female siblings.

Comment: This saying reflects the patrilineal nature of traditional Enuani society. However, there's an equivalent Enuani saying, *Ogoli bụ ụnọ*, meaning that the female child is the pillar of the home. Both sayings are used frequently as person names for newborn children.

❀ Okpoho tẹẹ njọ ofe ọ lacha-gbu ẹ

Literally: When the soup cooked by a woman turns out bad, she consumes it enthusiastically.

Figuratively: It is normal to promote something or someone that is yours, even if it's not that good.

Example: The tailor had made a bad mistake on Awele's jacket. One sleeve was longer than the other. But when Awele went to pick up the jacket, the tailor tried to minimize the gravity of the error. He tried to convince Awele that nobody would notice the difference in length, and that, in any case, there was a fashion line in London that flaunted asymmetrical clothing. Awele was not convinced, and took it simply as a case of **Okpoho...**

Comment: Spare a thought for the average woman in traditional Enuani society. Every night, and sometimes more frequently, she had to come up with a decent soup to go with the fufu meal. Quite often, the condiments were sparse, yet the expectation was for the outcome to be a masterpiece. She was raked with remorse each time the soup turned out bad.

✿ Ọkwụkwụ sị na ọ dị afụ ụfụ, ya huẹ nwammili ka anyị fụ

Literally: If the chicken says it's not difficult, let him urinate and let's see.

Figuratively: The person claiming that something is not difficult should prove their claim by performing the task. We should not make light of things that we cannot do. We should respect them instead.

Example: Awele managed to pass the professional exam that he took recently. But his workmate made light of the achievement, even though he himself had yet to study for and take the exam. Awele waited  patiently. If his workmate thought that the exam was a light matter, the proof would only come if the workmate scaled through it easily. **Ọkwụkwụ...**

Comment: A variant of this proverb is that if the chicken says it's not difficult, let him sprout teeth in his mouth: **Ọkwụkwụ sị na ọ dị afụ ụfụ, ya puẹ eze ka anyị fụ.**

✿ Ọlá mmanya mmadụ, madụ ga ala-kwa nke i?

Literally: You that are fond of drinking palm wine offered by other people, when will other people drink yours?

Figuratively: It is improper to exploit others. Generosity should never be in one direction only.

Example: One man in the village was noted for his appetite for parties. He attended every village event, eating and drinking at the expense of others. But he never hosted any of such events. When an altercation erupted between him and other villagers, they taunted him with the saying **Ọlá mmanya mmadụ, madụ ga ala-kwa nke i?**

Comment: The picture is one of a village vagrant who goes around drinking other people's palm wine, while rarely procuring palm wine for other people. Essentially, someone leeching off other people.

✺ Omè k'ọkẹlẹ, ya ji nkata je iyi

Literally: The hasty person goes to fetch water in the stream with a basket.

Figuratively: Too much haste can result in mistakes. Haste makes waste.

Example: In her hurry to get the children ready for school, the woman forgot the lunch that she had so carefully packed for them the night before. It was only after they reached the school that anyone noticed the error.

Comment: This is similar to the saying that too much hurry can result in a fall: **Gidigidi na ádá wị.**

✿ Ọnụ kwú njọ ga ekwu mma

Literally: The same person that speaks evil will ultimately speak good.

Figuratively: Your ill-wishers will ultimately turn around and become well-wishers. It is good to be patient with those who do not wish you well, since they could ultimately see the good in you.

Example: Awele had many opportunities to destroy the career of his adversarial workmate. But Awele chose to have patience, hoping that his workmate would ultimately see things better and maybe even become a well-wisher. **Ọnụ kwú...**

Comment: Patience with adversaries pays off in the end.

✿ Onye a-jụ njụ adị efuu ụzọ

Literally: The person that asks questions never gets lost.

Figuratively: Asking questions is the best way to expand your knowledge and stay on the right path.

Example: Awele was not fully familiar with the customs of his village. When he was about to perform the traditional wedding ceremony with his wife, he engaged his father in lengthy sessions, asking questions about all that was expected of him in the process. **Onye...**

Comment: Whether in the village, at work, or in academia, the habit of asking questions is the surest way for receiving guidance.

✿ Onye ála na uche ẹ wị

Literally: The mad person has his senses with him.

Figuratively: What might appear like madness may have some sense to it. There's sense to some madness; you only have to wait for the situation to clarify itself.

Example: City residents woke up one day to see one of the beautiful riverside buildings being demolished. The entire exercise appeared senseless, but the populace was willing to wait to see what was afoot. Unknown to them, this was to be the beachhead for a new bridge to be constructed across the river. Indeed, there was some sense to the madness. **Onye...**

Comment: Traditional Enuani society had very poor psychiatric care. Even though there were some traditional healers who dealt with such issues, most mentally disturbed people were ostracized and left to roam the streets.

✿ Onye any'isi sị na ya anụgaa kezię, ma wa ekezi-nę, ya aha-kọna

Literally: The blind man said that he heard a call for re-apportionment of the shared item, and he would refrain from taking his pick unless the sharing was adjusted.

Figuratively: One should be guided by the available knowledge unless and until better information comes along.

Example: A new pastor had been appointed for the village church. Weeks before he was to assume duty, a letter arrived claiming that the pastor had indulged in affairs with members of his congregation at his former post. Even though they lacked first-hand proof, the villagers immediately informed the bishop that they would not accept the new pastor. At least, not until the circumstances in his former post had been investigated and clarified. **Onye any'isi sị na ya anụgaa kezię, ma wa ekezi-nę, ya aha-kọna.**

Comment: The scenario indicated in this proverb is of the village gathering where some item (e.g. meat from a slaughtered animal) was being shared. The shares were usually arrayed on leaves spread on the ground, and people were invited in order of age seniority to make their pick. Occasionally, there would be an outcry that the shares were not equitable. The unseeing person, even though unable to see the evidence of uneven distribution, simply joined the chorus and insisted on re-distribution.

✿ Onye chọka nke dị azụ oziozi, nke dị ime ẹ ehufuẹ

Literally: If you fuss too much to lick the back of the ladle, the greater contents inside the ladle are likely to be spilled.

Figuratively: A greedy striving for the last bit of advantage can result in a total loss.

Example: Awele's uncle was known as a great yam farmer in the village. His yams easily out-yielded most other people. In an effort to press his advantage, he went and bought a special fertilizer that resulted in yet bigger yams. Unknown to him, this kind of fertilizer also resulted in rapid rotting of the harvested yams. Soon, his image in the village became tarnished. His effort to add to his already great fame had backfired on him. **Onye chọka…**

Comment: The traditional Enuani ladle, known as *Oziozi*, was a piece of long calabash that was dried and split in two to constitute two ladles. The volume inside each ladle was much more than that of any regular cooking spoon.…This proverb is similar to the one about the greedy caterpillar that ate up the leaves that were providing it with shade: **Ọbụbụ nwekẹ anya úkwú ọ tachapụụ akwụkwọ kpudoẹ ndo.** It is also similar to the saying that if you seek to have it all, you are at risk of losing it all: **Onye chọka nwa ncha, ọ yalị nwa ncha.**

✿ Onye chọka nwa ncha, ọ yalị nwa ncha

Literally: If you seek to have it all, you are at risk of losing it all.

Figuratively: Greed can backfire and lead to loss.

Example: The greedy young man in the city was eager to get rich quick. He dabbled in all kinds of business deals, some ethical and some not. Unfortunately, he got arrested for some of his unethical dealings, and now he's languishing in prison, much poorer than when he started off. **Onye...**

Comment: This is similar to the saying that fussing too much to get what's at the back of the ladle could result in spilling the contents of the ladle: **Onye chọka nke dị azụ oziozi, nke dị ime ẹ ehufuẹ.**

✿ Onye e-meli amusu ka ọ ta

Literally: It is the person who favors the witch that is haunted by the witch.

Figuratively: It is people closest to you that know enough about you to hurt you the most. Familiarity breeds contempt.

Example: When a serious burglary occurred in the village, everyone suspected that the gang must have deep inside knowledge about the village. Suspicions were confirmed when the police investigations implicated the son of one of the village chiefs. After all, **Onye...**

Comment: Traditional Enuani society had a strong belief in witchcraft. The witch, usually an elderly woman, was said to infect young children with witchcraft by giving them some food contaminated with witchcraft. The night owl was seen as an embodiment of witchcraft, and its haunting howls were dreaded by most villagers....This proverb is similar to the one about the dog that you cuddle being the one to start chewing on your clothing: **Wa patinye nwa nkite n'ahụ ọ takama ákwà.**

✿ Onye gbu ji lu mbá ga egwu ji lu mbá

Literally: The farmer that plants a big piece of yam will harvest a big tuber of yam.

Figuratively: As you sow, so you will reap. What you get out of a situation depends on what you put into it. Hard work results in plentiful reward and success.

Example: Awele's cousin was very hardworking and ambitious. She passed the professional exam well ahead of her mates and was very diligent at work. The managers appreciated her qualities and rewarded her with increased salary and rapid promotion. **Onye...**

Comment: In traditional Enuani society, the sheer size of each tuber in a man's yam harvest was a major factor in his prestige as a farmer. The surest way to realize big tubers was to plant with big seed tubers to start with.... This proverb is somewhat similar to the saying that the person who swallows the big fufu bolus will discharge the big chunk of excrement: **Onye lí nni gba okpi ga anyụ nsị gba okpi.**

❀ Onye isi awẹlẹ ya li azụ dị awaị

Literally: It's the lucky person that gets to eat the fish in the pottage as part of his portion.

Figuratively: It's a lucky person that gets favored by random chance.

Example: Awele's cousin frequently patronized the sports betting outlets. Awele tried his hand at such bets, but stopped after a string of stinging losses. His cousin never won big, but somehow she managed to win enough to cover her losses and keep going. Everyone regarded her as a lucky person in this regard. **Onye...**

Comment: Enuani pottage (*Awaị*) is prepared with yam, plantain or cocoyam, boiled together with vegetables, spices and palm oil. Fish (or meat) in the pottage is scanty, if at all. As portions of the pottage are shared out, nobody knows whose portion will have the one or two pieces of fish. Whoever gets the fish in their portion is indeed a lucky person.

✿ Onye kwei, chi ẹ ekwei

Literally: If you agree, your guardian spirit will also agree.

Figuratively: If you commit to an undertaking, you have to pursue it wholeheartedly, and you are likely to succeed. What you agree to is part of your destiny.

Example: Awele was scared of the thought that he had to build a house in the village. He did not feel capable of all that would be involved in the huge undertaking. However, his father convinced him that as a family man, he needed to brace up to the responsibility. He accepted the challenge and pursued it with relentless zeal, figuring that, **Onye...**

Comment: To the Enuani person, *Chi* is a sort of personal guardian angel which determines your destiny and guides you as the destiny plays out.

✿ Onye li nke nta ga eli nke úkwú

Literally: The person that eats the small one will ultimately get to eat the big one.

Figuratively: Be content and patient with small rewards, since bigger rewards may be waiting for you later. Bide your time.

Example: Awele's lottery-playing cousin usually won very small amounts. When people tried to persuade her to stop playing, she told them that her big winning might just be around the corner. Hopefully, the small winnings were only a prelude to some big ones. **Onye...**

Comment: Patience pays.

✿ Onye li nni gba okpi ga anyụ nsị gba okpi

Literally: The person that swallows the big fufu bolus will discharge a big chunk of excrement.

Figuratively: To whom much is given, much is expected.

Example: One of the businessmen from the village had reaped huge benefits from all kinds of support that the villagers gave him. They provided him cheap and sometimes free labor for his business, and gave him communal land to build his factory. When the village gathered to raise funds for the health center under construction, everyone looked up to this businessman to make a huge donation befitting his exalted stature and reflecting the community support he had received over the years. He did not disappoint. **Onye...**

Comment: One wonders if there is a biological basis to say that the size of the bolus determines the size of the excrement. But the saying sounds good and makes sense as a proverb ....This proverb is similar to the saying that the farmer who plants a big piece of yam will harvest a big tuber of yam: **Onye gbu ji lu mbá ga egwu ji lu mbá.**

✿ Onye na-agba ọgà na-alachakwa aka

Literally: The person sharing food at the village gathering is entitled to lick his fingers.

Figuratively: You should be free to enjoy the perks of your situation.

Example: To celebrate his chieftaincy installation, the village chief donated a huge batch of exercise books and stationery to the children at the primary school. The headmaster was responsible for distributing the items to the pupils. It turns out that the headmaster kept a portion of the goods for himself and the teachers, and the villagers saw nothing wrong with that. After all, **Onye...**

Comment: Whenever the village gathered to share cooked food (or a slaughtered animal), certain young men were tasked with the sharing duties. It was customary and expected for them to sequester small extra portions for themselves....A proverb with a similar implication is that the person playing the native horn is entitled to blow his nose: ***Onye na-egbu opi na-ezikwẹ imi.***

✿ Onye nyocha-ka ikè ọ fụ nsị

Literally: If you insist on examining the anus too intently, you're sure to find feces.

Figuratively: A stickler or nitpicker will always succeed in finding faults. If you insist on finding trouble, it's always there.

Example: When Awele's jobless cousin was living with him, the cousin usually stayed out till late at night. He gave the impression that he stayed late visiting prayer houses, but even at that, Awele wanted to stop the late night habit. His cousin actually stayed late visiting bars and brothels. Awele suspected as much, but took his cousin's explanation on face value. Awele was afraid of what he might find if he interrogated his cousin too closely. **Onye...**

Comment: This proverb is similar to the one that if you investigate a burrow too intently, you'll happen upon a snake: **Onye nyochaka ugbò ọ fụ agwọ.**

✿ Onye nyochaka ugbò ọ fụ agwọ

Literally: If you investigate a burrow too intently, you'll happen upon a snake.

Figuratively: The nitpicker out looking for a fault can always find one. It may be better to leave good enough alone. Be careful what you ask for or what you try to find out. It might be unpleasant.

Example: The village chief swore that he would not rest until he discovered who had been stealing ripe cocoa pods from his cocoa plantation. He told everybody about it. Such  petty thievery was common in the village farms, but the chief ignored the advice of most people to let the matter rest. Eventually, it was discovered that the chief's adolescent son had been leading a gang of petty thieves to steal and sell the cocoa. Now, the chief's family name was soiled, something that would not have happened if he had not been so intent on investigating and publicizing the petty theft. **Onye...**

Comment: Wandering around the farms and forests, the Enuani villager is likely to encounter burrows made by different animals. It is usual to stop to investigate these burrows for any edible animal that might be hiding there. Sometimes, the investigation turns up a hostile snake which is hiding there, even though it did not dig the burrow by itself.... This proverb is similar to the saying that if you look too intently at the anus, you're sure to find feces: **Onye nyochaka ikè ọ fụ nsị.**

✿ Onye taka ịta ọ tanye onye tanye ẹ nị

Literally: The avid gossiper unwittingly narrates a gossip to the person who told it to him in the first place.

Figuratively: The gossiper spreads gossip indiscriminately in all directions, including the direction of the origin of the gossip.

Example: A young villager rushed to the chief's house to tell him some hot news. Something that had never happened in the village had just happened: a woman had delivered triplets at the village maternity home. The chief acted surprised, although he had already heard the news. The new mother was actually his concubine, and he was the father of the children. It was he who should have been telling the visitor about the births, not the other way around.

Comment: In the absence of written or electronic sources of information, traditional Enuani society relied heavily on oral communication. The quality of such communication was always threatened by sheer gossip which sometimes tended to mix truth and falsehood.

❀ Onye tekẹ ntite o tee domeli oké

Literally: If you economize too much and hide away stuff, you might simply be hiding it where rats can ravage it.

Figuratively: Too much stinginess or economizing can sometimes be bad.

Example: The chief harvested a lot of corn from his farm. Most people sold their corn shortly after the harvest despite the prevailing low prices. But the chief wanted to hold his harvest for several months until the selling prices were higher. He stored the corn in large bins behind his house. Eventually, the selling prices did indeed rise, but when he opened the bins, he found that his corn had been devastated by weevils. It was hardly worth anything, certainly not worth selling, and he simply had to feed it to his chicken. **Onye…**

Comment: This is somewhat similar to the saying that while you insist on getting the perfect aim by pulling the bow repeatedly, the bird you're aiming at takes flight: **Wa dọtị-ka ụta nnụnụ efẹẹ.**

✿ Onye wa jụ adị ajụ onwe ẹ

Literally: If you are ostracized, you don't ostracize yourself. If the public rejects you, you don't reject yourself.

Figuratively: You should be confident in yourself, even if outsiders reject you.

Example: The businessman held a lavish Christmas party in the village each year. However, a few years ago, the village decided to ostracize him for his greedy habits. Since then, very few villagers attended his Christmas parties. But he persevered in staging the parties anyway, hoping that friends from other villages might make up the numbers. **Onye...**

Comment: This is similar to the Enuani proverb about the lizard that drops from a height praising himself since nobody around is praising him: **Ngwele si enu daa, ma wa ajana a ọ sị ka ya jaa onwe yẹ.**

❦ Onye zomekę ǫlịa ǫlịa ezome ę

Literally: If you hide an illness too much, the illness will eventually hide you.

Figuratively: If you hide your illness too much from those who can help you, the illness could ultimately hide you by causing your death.

Example: Some years ago, Awele's grandfather developed some unusual medical symptoms. His urination became frequent and strained. But he was too shy to let his relatives know, more so since the symptoms involved his genitalia. He was a couple of years into these symptoms before Awele got to know and took him to the doctor. The diagnosis was prostate cancer which by then had become too advanced to be treated. The man died a few months later. If the early symptoms had not been held as a secret, maybe something could have been done to save him. **Onye…**

Comment: It is wise to let relatives and health professionals know about your illness, since they are best positioned to help you.….In traditional Enuani society, illness was often handled secretly. More so since in many cases, the illness was ascribed to witchcraft or the doing of one's enemies.

✿ Ọsa enwenẹ ákwụ́, ma ashịa enwenẹ ákwụ́, mana wa ekpoli ọgwụ n'enu nkwụ

Literally: Neither the squirrel nor the weaver bird owns the oil palm fruit, but they are fighting over it on top of the palm tree.

Figuratively: In life, there are many situations when two parties fight over an item that rightly belongs to neither of them.

Example: The Irish Roman Catholics and the English Anglicans were engaged in a fierce battle for souls in colonial Enuani. By right, the territory belonged to neither of them, but they positioned themselves to fight over it.

Comment: Enuani villagers are witness to frequent fights between the squirrel and the weaver bird, as they wrestle each other for the palm fruits on top of the palm tree.

✿ Oshi zu egede, bei ka ọ nọ ti ẹ?

Literally: For the thief that steals a drum, where will he beat it?

Figuratively: Only a fool steals an object that is easily traceable; or indulges in a malpractice that is easy to detect.

Example: Awele's corrupt boss had amassed quite some wealth. But he was afraid that the anti-corruption agency would be on his trail if he invested the money or used it to build a mansion. So, he kept much of the money with friends while he tried to figure out how to spend it. **Oshi...**

Comment: Drums and other percussions were the main musical instruments in traditional Enuani. The only major wind instrument was the *Akpẹlẹ*, a small elongated gourd with a perforation in it. The locally-made bamboo flute, *Ọjà*, became popular during colonial times, but hardly ever featured in traditional music. The bone flute (*Opi*), so popular east of the Niger, was uncommon in traditional Enuani.

🌀 Ote égwú adị agọsị sọ ofu onye ikè

Literally: The traditional dancer does not point the rear end at only one person.

Figuratively: Someone's bad character can be detected by multiple people.

Example: Awele's jobless cousin liked the night life of the city. This caused him to fall out with Awele. He then moved out and went to live with another cousin. There too, he ran into trouble for the same reasons and was forced to move out again. His third host has already started grumbling and may kick him out soon. He's showing his bad character to all the various relatives. **Ote...**

Comment: This proverb is most often used in a negative sense where a person's bad character is manifesting to numerous people. A variant of this proverb is that the person who is sweeping the compound does not point the rear end at only one person: *Ọza ezi adị agọsị sọ ofu onye ikè.*

❀ Ọyị ewii na ụgbaà, oke nnọchime na-ebuhẹ esemokwu

Literally: The friendship of the rabbit and the oilbean tree, too much closeness can bring discord.

Figuratively: Too much closeness can destroy a relationship. The parties must allow each other breathing room. Familiarity breeds contempt.

Example: When Awele lived apart from his cousin, they related nicely with each other. But the situation changed when the cousin came to live with Awele in the city. They quarreled often. Increased physical closeness had destroyed their relationship, just like the rabbit and the oilbean tree.

Comment: The legend of the rabbit and the oilbean tree runs as follows. The friendship between the rabbit and the tree flourished while the rabbit had its burrow some distance away, and enjoyed the oilbean seeds that were explosively dispersed to the burrow. Then the rabbit tried to escalate the friendship by coming closer and burrowing right under the tree. The tree became angry that its roots were being destroyed by burrowing, while the rabbit angrily watched the seeds being flung far from its new burrow home. Too much closeness destroyed the friendship....Like the rabbit, Enuani people love the oilbean seeds (*Ugba*à). The seeds, dispersed explosively from the tree, are collected, boiled, sliced and allowed to ferment for a few days. The result is a delicious condiment, used in soups and other delicacies.

❦ Ozi adị egbu ụkọ

Literally: The message does not kill the messenger.

Figuratively: Conveying the message should not pose harm to the messenger.

Example: The junior workers in one section of the company met and decided that they needed an upgrade in their work stations. They conveyed this request to the section manager, who in turn was to convey it to the general manager. But the section manager was reluctant since he was aware of the recent financial difficulties in the company. To overcome his reluctance, the workers reminded him that he was only conveying their message to the upper management. After all, **Ozi...**

Comment: This proverb is similar to the one saying that while the head did not utter the offending fart, *it* receives the punitive knock: **Isi anyụna ahụlụ mana o bulu ọkpọ.**

❀ Ozu si-me ọyị ana-a

Literally: When the corpse starts to stink, friends go home (while the relatives persevere and go through with the burial).

Figuratively: When things go bad, friends may abandon you, but your blood relatives stick with you through thick and thin.

Example: Awele's aunt was rich and prosperous earlier in her life. At that time, she had numerous friends hanging around to enjoy her riches with her. But when she fell on hard times and became sickly, most of those friends deserted her. Only Awele and a couple of relatives stuck with her and supported her in her travails. The previous friends were nowhere to be found because, **Ozu...**

Comment: With no refrigeration facilities in traditional Enuani, managing a corpse was a huge challenge. Despite traditional potions administered to stave off decay, most corpses were barely presentable by the third or fourth day after death. Interments were therefore arranged with all due haste.

❀ Sọ osisi dị ọfịa ka wa ga agwa na wa aga egbu ẹ, ọ kwụlụ be ọ kwụ

Literally: It is only a tree that stays put where it is standing, after being told that it is about to be cut down.

Figuratively: Humans are expected to take defensive action if they are forewarned of imminent danger. They don't just stand there.

Example: Awele was well aware of the secret ploy of his malicious workmate to get him fired. He figured it would be prudent of him not to sit idle and watch his workmate's evil plans succeed. So, Awele rose to the occasion and instituted his own measures to counter the plan of his workmate. Having been forewarned, he was wise not to be a spectator to his own demise. He took action knowing that, **Sọ osisi...**

Comment: Fight or flight in the presence of danger is a normal reaction among humans and animals. Inaction is rarely the response.

✽ Ụla emebinẹ anya

Literally: Sleep does not harm the eyes.

Figuratively: Certain things have their place and purpose. Some things that may seem alarming may indeed do no harm.

Example: Awele was all worked up that someone had set traps inside his village plot of land, apparently prospecting for bush meat. He complained to his father with some alarm about the apparent trespass. His father assured him that such a minor encroachment did not represent a counterclaim to the plot, and was normal practice in the village. In any case, the infraction did not prevent Awele from proceeding with his own plans for the plot. After all, **Ụla...**

Comment: This proverb is most often used when an apparent threat is indeed harmless or when things have gone as expected.

✿ Ụnọ ka iwe dị

Literally: Home is where enmity dwells.

Figuratively: The bitterest conflicts are those that arise between close relatives.

Example: Two of Awele's uncles had a falling out over which of them deserved to be the next chief. The disagreement spread to the respective families of the two men. There was mutual suspicion that poisoning and witchcraft were being employed in the dispute. They dragged each other through all the conflict resolution processes in the village. Despite entreaties from outsiders, one of the men has now hired a lawyer and is pursuing the matter through the law courts. Despite their being blood relatives, the bitterness between the parties has remained extremely potent, defying resolution.

Comment: Various forms of this saying are sometimes given as person names to newborn babies….This proverb is similar to the saying that the dog that you cuddle is the one that starts chewing on your clothing: **Wa patinye nwa nkite n'ahụ ọ takama ákwà.**

❀ Ụtọmị na awẹlẹ

Literally: Long life and good fortune.

Figuratively: Long life and prosperity.

Example: When Awele's father visited the chief, the chief presented him with kolanuts. When the chief was breaking the kolanuts, his main invocation for all present was, **Utọmị...**

Comment: This saying is used for wishing persons well either on special occasions or at random encounters.

✿ Ụzọ teẹ nte ma njọ adịna a

Literally: A long route is acceptable so long as no harm lurks in it.

Figuratively: The lengthy option devoid of peril is always preferable to the shortcut that may pose some danger.

Example: Awele started courting his girlfriend when she was still a student at the university. He was ready to marry and she was willing. He contemplated approaching  her father with a marriage offer. But she confided in him that her father had sworn not to entertain any marriage offers until she had finished at the university. Rather than risk alienating the father with a precipitous marriage offer, the couple chose to wait till she finished schooling. It was a longer route, but it promised a safer result. After all, **Ụzọ...**

Comment: Slow but sure is preferable to fast and insecure. Slow and steady wins the race.

Wa adị afụ ọnụ anị ji la mmili

Literally: You cannot see the mouth that the soil uses to drink water.

Figuratively: Some things disappear mysteriously, just as water poured on the soil.

Example: Despite his devious corrupt practices, Awele's boss was careful to cover his tracks carefully. Hardly anybody knew how he came by his riches. It was a case of, **Wa adị afụ...**

Comment: This saying is used when something happens inexplicably or disappears mysteriously.

ꙮ Wa adị ahapụ isi aka agba ụlịọ

Literally: You cannot snap your fingers without the thumb.

Figuratively: You cannot undertake an exercise in the absence of a key element in the process.

Example: Awele gathered his relatives to pay a formal "wine carrying" visit to his fiancée's uncle living just across town in the city. The uncle received them well. However, he made it clear that he had no authority to give his family's blessing to a possible union between Awele and the girl. Such authority resided exclusively with their chief in the village, many miles away. They were advised to repeat the formal visit, this time at the chief's house. You cannot bypass the chief because, **Wa adị...**

Comment: This is similar to the saying that yam does not sprout from the tail end: **Ji adị esi ọdụ` epu.**

❀ Wa adị ama akankwụ ga elu ugbó

Literally: You never know which ignited firewood ember will make it to the farm.

Figuratively: You never know which items will survive adversity, so you better hedge your bets. Don't put all your eggs in one basket.

Example: Awele was conflicted as to which companies to buy shares in, given recent market fluctuations. So, he decided to spread his risk by buying small amounts in each of several companies. You never know which companies will go bust, and which ones will boom in the long run. **Wa adị...**

Comment: The farm workday in the traditional Enuani society started with the building of a cooking fire in one corner of the farm. This fire would be used later for boiling or roasting yams as the midday meal. Farms were often located a mile or two from the home. Since fire-making safety matches were unknown at the time, an ignited piece of firewood (*Akankwụ*) from the home fire had to be carried all the way to the farm. The person with the ember had to carefully nurse the fire to ensure that the fire made it to the farm. On occasion, to the frustration of all concerned, the fire on the firewood died out before getting to the farm. Hence the saying, **Wa adị...**

❀ Wa adị anọọ ofu etiti ekili egwu

Literally: You don't stand on one spot to watch the dancing.

Figuratively: You need to shift around your position and strategies as the occasion demands.

Example: Even though his current job was good enough, Awele took the advice of his friends that he should continue to look around the job market for possible better prospects. It would be unwise for him to sit contentedly on his current job. He needed to be looking around. After all, **Wa adị...**

Comment: Traditional dancing in Enuani was typically performed in an outdoor setting. Most of the spectators remained standing, milling excitedly around the dancing location. To get the best views, it was often necessary to shift your location every few minutes.

✿ Wa adị ebu iwe elu mmọ

Literally: You don't nurse anger or enmity into the spirit world.

Figuratively: Certain grave events can cause you to suspend your anger or enmity.

Example: Awele seriously disliked his malicious workmate, and the two hardly ever socialized. They certainly did not exchange home visits. But misfortune struck the workmate suddenly. One of his sons died in a freak car accident. Despite the long-standing dislike, Awele felt obliged to pay a solemn condolence visit to the workmate at his home. He figured that, **Wa adị...**

Comment: Enuani traditional religion holds that everybody goes to the spirit world after they die. Ancestors inhabiting the spirit world can be the objects of supplication and worship.

✿ Wa adị eji ife wa ji agba ntị agba anya

Literally: The tool you use to clean the ear would be improper for cleaning the eyes.

Figuratively: Each situation has certain measures that are suited to it. The right remedy applied to the wrong ailment gives bad results.

Example: Awele's auntie stubbed her toe and was effectively treated at the village health center. Indeed her many minor ailments were effectively treated at the same facility. When she suddenly developed heart palpitations, she wanted to go to the same health center for attention. But Awele advised her that the heart ailment was of a different order of seriousness from her previous ailments. It required the attention of a specialist doctor in the city hospital. The village health center was unsuitable because, **Wa adị...**

Comment: In traditional Enuani, the tool of choice for cleaning the ear was the tip of a feather.

❦ Wa afụ ngịlịafọ ofu ụbọsị, sị ka wa numinẹ ẹ?

Literally: You see the intestine on just one occasion, then ask for it to be pushed back in?

Figuratively: When a good rare event occurs, why keep it short? Why not prolong the enjoyment of it?

Example: Awele's childhood friend was visiting home on vacation from America. Since his vacation was short, he planned to spend only one day with Awele. But Awele pleaded with his friend to apportion a couple of more days for them to be together. Since they had not seen each other for years, why not prolong the stay? **Wa afụ...**

Comment: This proverb is somewhat bizarre since it refers to a human intestine coming into view outside a medical facility. Surprisingly, the proverb occurs fairly frequently in Enuani diction. It is used for situations where a pleasant but rare event is liable to being shortened or terminated.... This proverb is usually rendered as a question, but it could also be spoken as a statement.

✿ Wa dọtị-ka ụta nnụnụ efẹẹ

Literally: When you waste time trying to get the perfect aim by pulling the bowstring repeatedly, the bird you're aiming at takes flight.

Figuratively: Too much craftiness and fine-tuning can sometimes lead to lost opportunities.

Example: Awele had a sum of money that he wanted to invest in the stock market. Since prices on the market had been falling for some months, he wanted to wait till the market hit rock bottom. Then, in the first week of June, the market went up; but Awele was not concerned since it had done so before, only to continue its downward slide. In the second week of June, the market went up again; and again Awele thought the rise was a fluke. In the third week, the market went up even more steeply than before. Now Awele was in a bind. Should he continue waiting for further falls in the market? Eventually, he had to invest at the new higher prices. His long wait to fine-tune his timing had resulted in a lost opportunity. It was a case of, **Wa dọtịka...**

Comment: This is somewhat similar to the saying that if you economize too much and hide away stuff, you might simply be hiding it where rats can ravage it: **Onye tekẹ ntite o tee domeli oké.**

❀ Wa hukọma nwammili ọnụ, ọ gbọa ụfụfọ

Literally: When you focus your urinating on the same spot, that is when you get it to foam.

Figuratively: Focusing effort on the same purpose is the surest way to achieve success. Dispersed effort is wasteful.

Example: Since Awele's village was not connected to the electricity grid, many of the wealthy villagers simply procured individual electricity generators for their homes. But at the village meeting, some wise folks advocated that the effort used to acquire and operate individual generators could best be pooled to work towards electrifying the entire village. They buttressed their argument by saying that dispersed individual effort was less efficient than collective community effort: **Wa...**

Comment: Since there was no indoor plumbing in traditional Enuani society, urinating outdoors was the norm.

✿ Wa linashị onye nweni idumu ànụ́

Literally: When the owner of something is cheated by being assigned a minority share, the entire village will hear about it.

Figuratively: The victim of inequity is justified to raise an alarm.

Example: To try to balance their budgets, both the state and the local government had raised taxes and instituted all kinds of levies. It was as if a huge chunk of each person's paycheck was being taken in taxes and levies. Eventually, some people organized a demonstration to protest the high deductions from their salaries. The salary was theirs, but the government seemed to be taking a disproportionate bite out of it. Time to raise an alarm. **Wa linashị...**

Comment: This is similar to the proverb wishing that the visitor not take over your abode: **Ọbịa be onye abịágbúnẹ ẹ.**

✿ Wa megbukẹ nwata wa ezi ẹ ịka ahụ

Literally: If you maltreat a child too much, you toughen him up to persevere.

Figuratively: Adversity inures you and leads to resilience. What does not kill you makes you stronger.

Example: For years, a merchant from the city came to the village to buy up all the produce. Everybody knew that he was cheating the villagers by buying at very low prices from them. But he was the only merchant and had a monopoly to buy at whatever price he dictated. Having been cheated this way for years, the villagers eventually got smart and deliberately sought out other merchants to come to the village to compete for their produce. The competition paid off and the selling prices for their produce improved considerably. The initial maltreatment by one merchant had stirred them into useful action. **Wa megbukẹ...**

Comment: In traditional Enuani society, it was commonplace for children to be fostered out to relatives or friends. The presumption was that living with the parents led to pampering, while living with others presented a tougher situation that led to resilience.

✿ Wa n'ákwá akpa maka ife ogonogo, gbụẹ agwọ chịlị a n'aka?

Literally: Do you sew a bag for lengthy items, then carry a killed snake on your hands?

Figuratively: Do you go to the trouble of fashioning an item, then ignore it when it should be used?

Example: The village health center was built to help improve health care in the village. It was intended to reduce the reliance on traditional healers whose practices were sometimes ineffective. But several years after it was established, the health center was being patronized by very few people. They still took their ailments to the traditional healers. The function which the health center was set up to perform was still being diverted to other avenues. The government which established the health center could only wonder, **Wa...**

Comment: In traditional Enuani, most snakes were considered fair game for their meat. Usually, snakes killed or caught in traps, were first decapitated. The head, containing the venom, was buried, while the rest of the snake was carried in a bag....This proverb is usually rendered as a question, but it could also be spoken as a statement.

✿ Wa n'enii onye mmili gbu, ndi n'eni ẹ ni alakwa mmili

Literally: While burying the person that died of drowning, the mourners still drink water.

Figuratively: A thing that is a friend in one situation can turn out to be a foe in another situation.

Example: When some villagers proposed to electrify the whole village, one elderly man objected, saying that he heard that electricity can shock people to death. Some of the younger villagers tried to reassure him that even though electricity can cause harm, it has numerous advantages. We try to enjoy its advantages while coping with its dangers.

Comment: This proverb points out the paradox that water can be a friend or a foe, depending on the situation. While some are desperately praying for rain, others are frantically fleeing from floods. The same water. A similar thing can be said of electricity.

✿ Wa patinye nwa nkite n'ahụ ọ takama ákwà

Literally: The dog that you cuddle is the one that starts chewing on your clothing.

Figuratively: People closest to you are the ones that can hurt you the most. Familiarity breeds contempt.

Example: Awele allowed one of his cousins to squat in a room in his village house. A couple of months later, Awele noticed that his cousin had brought a friend of his to live there too. Moreover, they had  converted the premises into a virtual mechanic workshop for their two motorcycles. Awele regretted letting his cousin live there in the first place. **Wa patinye...**

Comment: This is similar to the saying that it is the person who favors the witch that is haunted by the witch: **Onye e-meli amusu ka ọ ta.** It is also similar to the one about home being where enmity dwells: **Ụnọ ka iwe dị,** and to the proverb wishing that the stranger may not take over your home: **Ọbịa be onye abịágbúnẹ ẹ.**

Appendix

Map of Nigeria showing approximate location of Enuani

Other books by Prof. Inno Chukuma ONWUEME

[Search with title or author name at Amazon, Google Books, Barnes & Noble, etc.]

1. Questions Not Being Asked: Topical philosophical critiques in prose, proverbs, and poems. Author House 2015. 206pp. [Readers' Favorite Five star winner 2015].

2. Like A Lily Among Thorns: Colonial African village child transitions to post-colonial modernity, and America. Author House 2014. 348pp. [Readers' Favorite FIVE-STAR winner 2014].

3. Auction In Zunguzonga: Sustainable Development Deferred. Author House, 2005. 206pp.

4. Okita Okita: Tales about Anioma culture in Africa. 1st Books Publishers, 2001. 104pp. [Winner, *Writer's Digest* MERIT AWARD, 2002]

5. Taro cultivation in Asia and the Pacific. FAO (United Nations Food & Agricultural Organization) RAP Publication: 1999/16.

6. The kava crop and its potential. United Nations FAO, RAP Publication 1997/12. [with M.Papademetriou]

7. Tropical Root and Tuber Crops: Production, Perspectives, and Future Prospects. United Nations FAO, Rome. 1994. 228pp. [with W.B.Charles]

8. Agrometeorology and Eco-physiology of Cassava. Monograph for the World Meteorological Organization, Geneva, Switzerland. 1993

9. Field Crop Production in Tropical Africa. CTA, Wageningen, Netherlands. 1991. 480pp. [with T.D.Sinha]

10. General Agriculture & Soils. (editor). Cassell Ltd. London. 1982. 102pp. [with E.A.Aduayi & E.E.Ekong]

11. Animal Science. (editor) Cassell Ltd. London 1981. 105pp. [with G.Ositelu]

12. Crop Science. Cassell Ltd. London. 1979. 106pp.

13. The Tropical Tuber Crops: yams, cassava, sweet potato, cocoyams. John Wiley & Sons, Chichester, UK. 1978. 234pp.

Enuani Resources (Selected References and Links)

enuaniculture.com

enuaniculture.org

enuani.com

https://www.uniprojectmaterials.com/african-languages/
project-topics/wh-question-in-akwukwu-igbo-dialect-of-igbo

http://www.ibusa.net/enuani%20-%20ibusa.htm

https://www.revolvy.com/main/index.php?s=Enuani+dialect

https://www.researchgate.net/publication/238114585_
Origins and Migrations of the Enuani People of South
Central Nigeria Reconsidered

http://enacademic.com/dic.nsf/enwiki/11204058

https://uniprojectmaterials.com/african-languages/
comparative-study-of-enuani-and-he-nkwerre-dialect-
of-igbo-language/project-topics-materials-for-final-year-
students

http://enacademic.com/dic.nsf/enwiki/11204058

https://ipfs.io/ipfs/QmXoypizjW3WknFiJnKLwHCnL
72vedxjQkDDP1mXWo6uco/wiki/Enuani dialect.html

https://www.tandfonline.com/doi/abs/10.1080/0972639X.2012.
11886643

❖ **Did you know that in traditional Enuani society:**
  - Yam was the noble crop, complete with its own god and festivals
  - Men did most of the farming while women did most of the produce processing and marketing
  - Plant products of greatest cultural significance were yam, kolanuts, and palm wine
  - Time was reckoned in a repeating cycle of four named days, not seven
  - Land was owned communally, with allowance made for individual *use*
  - Children's treats included at least four kinds of edible insects
  - Proverbs were used extensively in speech and storytelling
  - Justice in each community was dispensed by a standing committee, often called *Onotu*

❖ What else don't you know about this vibrant culture? This book, *ENUANI*, invites you to find out. Welcome!

(See back cover for information About the Authors)

❖ **Lift the veil on Enuani African tradition with culture-dense tales, essays, and proverbs. Witness a culture in the throes of transition to modernity. Compelling, instructive, entertaining and captivating...**

❖ **Accolades for previous books by Inno Onwueme:**

- "...an excellent memoir... With superb narrative skills reminiscent of those his countryman Wole Soyinka used in his own autobiography." – John E Roper of *US Review of Books*, reviewing *Like a Lily Among Thorns*.

- "...The writing style is fluid, simple, and genuine...a book that left me thinking long after I finished it, and one that I will be re-reading for a long time to come," – Gisela Dixon of *Readers Favorite*, reviewing *Questions Not Being Asked*.

- "...polished and professional... an incredible story... well organized." – *Writers Digest* reviewing *Like a Lily Among Thorns*

- "...Wow! That's what I thought when I got through reading *Questions Not Being Asked*... a very intriguing read." – Tracy A. Fischer.

Printed in the United States
By Bookmasters